Grade

3

the [Visual] Guide to Third Grade

Thinking Kids™
An imprint of Carson-Dellosa Publishing LLC
P.O. Box 35665
Greensboro, NC 27425 USA

Thinking Kids™
An imprint of Carson-Dellosa Publishing LLC
P.O. Box 35665
Greensboro, NC 27425 USA

© 2016 Carson-Dellosa Publishing LLC. Except as permitted under the United States Copyright Act, no part of this publication may be reproduced, stored, or distributed in any form or by any means (mechanically, electronically, recording, etc.) without the prior written consent of Carson-Dellosa Publishing LLC. Thinking Kids™ is an imprint of Carson-Dellosa Publishing LLC.

Printed in the USA • All rights reserved.
01-060167784

ISBN 978-1-4838-2684-4

Infographics and Learning Activities

That's Loud!

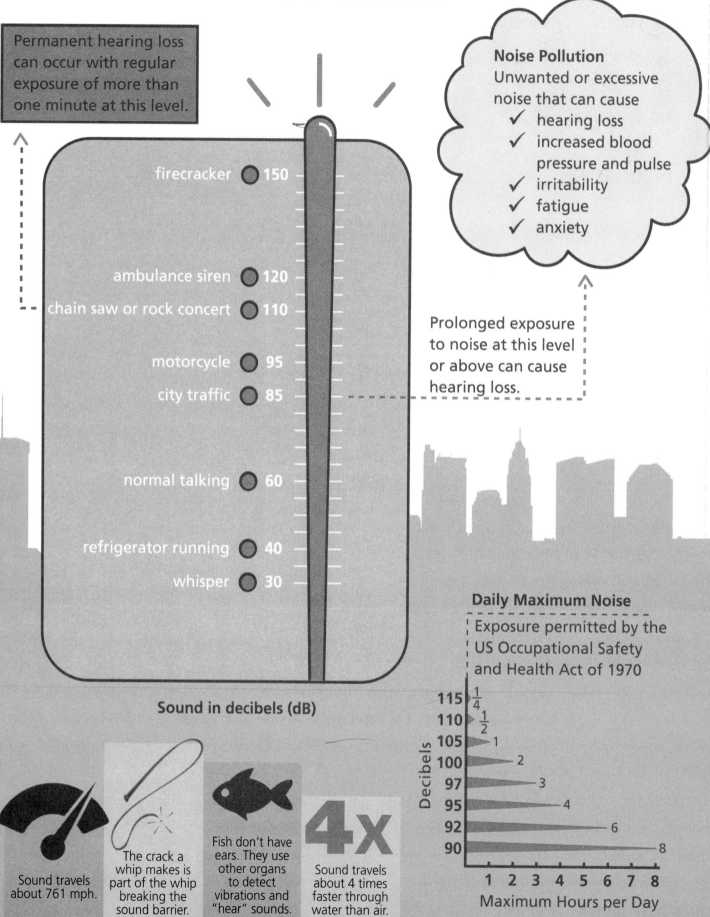

Permanent hearing loss can occur with regular exposure of more than one minute at this level.

Noise Pollution
Unwanted or excessive noise that can cause
- ✓ hearing loss
- ✓ increased blood pressure and pulse
- ✓ irritability
- ✓ fatigue
- ✓ anxiety

firecracker	150
ambulance siren	120
chain saw or rock concert	110
motorcycle	95
city traffic	85
normal talking	60
refrigerator running	40
whisper	30

Prolonged exposure to noise at this level or above can cause hearing loss.

Sound in decibels (dB)

Daily Maximum Noise
Exposure permitted by the US Occupational Safety and Health Act of 1970

Decibels	Maximum Hours per Day
115	$\frac{1}{4}$
110	$\frac{1}{2}$
105	1
100	2
97	3
95	4
92	6
90	8

Sound travels about 761 mph.

The crack a whip makes is part of the whip breaking the sound barrier.

Fish don't have ears. They use other organs to detect vibrations and "hear" sounds.

4x Sound travels about 4 times faster through water than air.

Think and Solve

Study the infographic. Answer the questions.

1. How many more decibels louder is an ambulance siren than a refrigerator?

A. 140 dB

B. 120 dB

C. 80 dB *(circled)*

D. 100 dB

(handwritten:)
```
  120      40
-  40
 ───
   80
```

2. The noise of a circular saw is 100 decibels. According to the US Occupational Safety and Health Act of 1970, what is the maximum number of hours a day you should use a circular saw?

_____ 2 hr _____

3. Prolonged exposure to city traffic can cause hearing loss.

(**True**) *(circled)*   **False**

4. Give an example of noise pollution. Explain why the noise is a kind of pollution.

_____

_____

5. Where do you think the sound of a rocket launch would be placed on the graph?

_____

_____

Estimate It

Go outside and listen. What do you hear? List the sounds on the lines.
Color the bar to estimate the decibels for each sound.

dishwasher

talking

fridge

giggles

DECIBELS   5 15 25 35 45 55 65 75 85 95 105 115 125 135 150

Greenback Facts

Before you spend your money . . . slow down! Take a closer look at US currency.

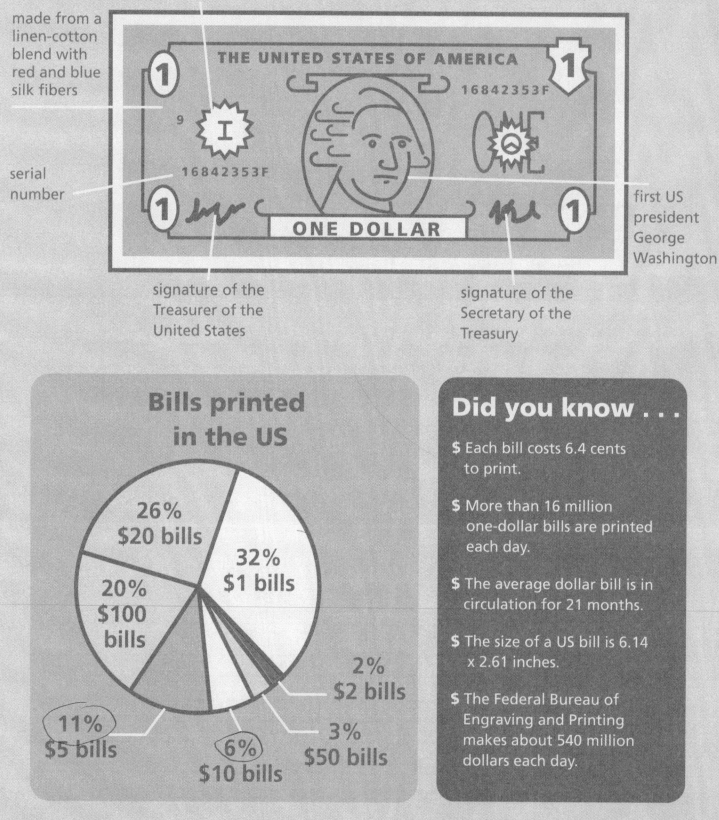

code for Federal Reserve Bank that ordered the bill (I = Minneapolis)

made from a linen-cotton blend with red and blue silk fibers

serial number

THE UNITED STATES OF AMERICA

1 16842353F

9

I

16842353F

ONE DOLLAR

signature of the Treasurer of the United States

signature of the Secretary of the Treasury

first US president George Washington

Bills printed in the US

26% $20 bills

32% $1 bills

20% $100 bills

11% $5 bills

6% $10 bills

3% $50 bills

2% $2 bills

Did you know . . .

$ Each bill costs 6.4 cents to print.

$ More than 16 million one-dollar bills are printed each day.

$ The average dollar bill is in circulation for 21 months.

$ The size of a US bill is 6.14 x 2.61 inches.

$ The Federal Bureau of Engraving and Printing makes about 540 million dollars each day.

E Pluribus Unum means "out of many, one" in Latin

THE UNITED STATES OF AMERICA

ONE

ONE

175

ONE DOLLAR

the bald eagle is the symbol on the Great Seal of the United States

Roman numerals for 1776

Novus Ordo Seclorum
means "new order of the ages" in Latin

plate serial number

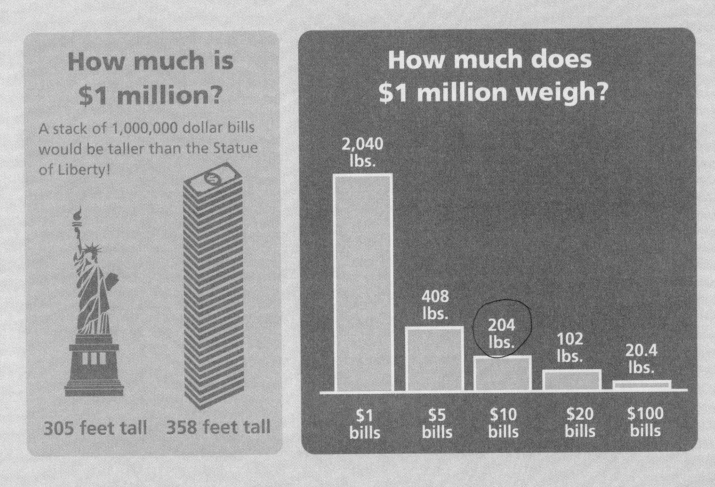

How much is $1 million?

A stack of 1,000,000 dollar bills would be taller than the Statue of Liberty!

305 feet tall   358 feet tall

How much does $1 million weigh?

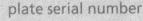

2,040 lbs.

408 lbs.

204 lbs.

102 lbs.

20.4 lbs.

| $1 bills | $5 bills | $10 bills | $20 bills | $100 bills |

Do the Math

Study the infographic. Solve the problems.

1. How much taller would a stack of 2,000,000 dollar bills be than the Statue of Liberty?

   A. 53 feet

   B. 106 feet

   C. 252 feet

   D. 411 feet

   (handwritten work, right margin:)
   $$\begin{array}{r} 1 \\ 358 \\ +358 \\ \hline 716 \\ -305 \\ \hline 411 \end{array}$$

2. About how many one-dollar bills are printed in five days?

   A. 16 million

   B. 48 million

   C. 64 million

   D. 80 million

   (handwritten work:)
   $$\begin{array}{r} 16 \\ \times\ 5 \\ \hline 80 \end{array}$$

   $$\begin{array}{r} 16 \\ 16 \\ 16 \\ 16 \\ 16 \\ \hline \end{array}$$

3. What percentage of bills printed in the US are five- and ten-dollar bills?

   _____ 17% _____

4. How much less does one million dollars weigh in ten-dollar bills than in one-dollar bills?

   (handwritten work, right margin:)
   $$\begin{array}{r} 2040 \\ -\ 204 \\ \hline 1,836\ \text{lb} \end{array}$$

   _____

5. Is the average dollar bill in circulation for more or (less) than two years?

   _____

Make a Chart

Gather five different coins and bills. Look at the money carefully, noticing details. Then, use the chart below to record information about each coin or bill. Write its value, the date that appears on it, the name of the person whose portrait appears on it, and one more detail.

Money Type	Value	Date	Portrait	Another Detail

Make a Plan

Maybe you want to buy a new bike, but it is expensive. Or, you want to give a generous amount of money to an animal shelter. Maybe you want to buy a gift for your brother, but the item he wants costs more than what you get for a weekly allowance.

The answer is saving! If you save a little each week, it can add up to a lot of money over time. Use the chart below to set a savings goal and make a plan to reach that goal.

What do you want to save for? _house for kids_

You have 12 weeks to save. How much money do you want to have at the end of 12 weeks? _$2,000_

How much do you need to save each week to reach your goal? _____

Record this amount for each week in the column *Weekly Savings Goal* below. In the next column, record the amount you actually saved. Keep a running total of what you have saved so far in the last column.

	Weekly Savings Goal	How Much I Saved	Total Saved
Week 1	166		
Week 2	166		
Week 3	166		
Week 4	166		
Week 5	166		
Week 6	166		
Week 7	166		
Week 8	166		
Week 9	166		
Week 10	166		
Week 11	166		
Week 12	166		

Did you reach your goal? _____

What did you learn about saving money? _____

_____

$$166$$
$$2,000 \div 12$$
$$12$$
$$80$$
$$72$$
$$= 80$$

$$12 \times 6 = 72$$

The Iditarod

Each March, mushers and their dogs compete in a sled-dog race across Alaska. The Iditarod has been called "The Last Great Race on Earth."

MARCH						
SUN.	MON.	TUE.	WED.	THUR.	FRI.	SAT.
				1	2	3 Anchorage
Willow 4	5	6	7	Huslia or Eagle Island 8	9	10
11	12	13	Nome (about 985 miles) 14	15	16	17

At some point during the race, mushers must make a mandatory, 24-hour stop to rest.

The race begins on the first Saturday in March. An average of 65 teams begin the race each year.

After the symbolic start in Anchorage, mushers line up for a restart in Willow. The official race clock begins.

Mushers reach the halfway mark (about 490 miles) at the checkpoint in Huslia (northern route) or Eagle Island (southern route). The routes alternate each year.

Mushers arrive at the finish line in Nome 9 to 12 days after the restart in Willow. Dallas Seavey set a race record in 2014 with a time of 8 days, 13 hours, 4 minutes, and 19 seconds.

Twice in its 43-year history (in 2003 and 2015), the race start has moved to Fairbanks due to unseasonably warm weather and a lack of snow.

Alaska

Northern Route (Even Years)

Nome

Southern Route (Odd Years)

Anchorage

The Great Race of Mercy

Sled teams delivered mail and supplies to such towns as Nome, Alaska, and Iditarod, Alaska, in the early 1920s. But with the invention of the airplane, dogsleds were no longer the main means of crossing the dangerous terrain. However, in 1925, there was an outbreak of a terrible illness called *diphtheria*. Nome's only doctor knew that he needed a serum to treat the sick and to keep the disease from spreading. The only way to get the serum to Nome in the rough winter weather was by dogsled. A team of the best dogs and mushers was hastily put together. They carried the serum from Nenana, Alaska, to Nome, Alaska, in a record 5 days and 7 hours. The trip usually took 15 to 20 days! Countless lives were saved as a result of some very brave dogs and their mushers. Today, the Iditarod Trail Race is held each year to honor this historic journey.

Dogsled Commands

Gee: Turn right
Haw: Turn left
Mush: Go
Line out: Lead dog, pull ahead
Whoa: Stop
Easy: Slow down
On by: Keep moving forward
Come gee/Come haw:
Turn in the opposite direction

Think and Solve
Study the infographic. Answer the questions.

1. What does the dog sled command *easy* mean?

    A. turn right

    B. turn left

    C. slow down

    D. stop

2. If a race team is racing on the southern route, where is the halfway checkpoint?

    _____

3. What happened during the Great Race of Mercy?

    A. A team of mushers delivered medicine to Nome, Alaska, in rough winter weather.

    B. A team of mushers had to deliver mail to Willow, Alaska, in icy conditions.

    C. A team of mushers raced each other to win money for a charity.

    D. none of the above

4. Diphtheria is a type of _____.

5. Would you like to be on a race team in the Iditarod? Why or why not?

    _____

    _____

Write About It
Imagine that you are a contestant in the Iditarod. Write a journal entry about your experience on one day of the race.

_____

_____

_____

_____

_____

Piece It Together

Cut out the labels at the bottom of the page. Use the clues below to glue or tape the labels in the correct places on the map on page 17. The map shows the serum route from Nenana, Alaska, to Nome, Alaska, during the Great Race of Mercy.

❄ **Minto is the first town the musher and dogs would arrive at after leaving Nenana.**

❄ **Nine Mile Cabin is between Kokrines and Kallands.**

❄ **Unalakleet is to the west of Old Woman Cabin.**

❄ **Port Safety is the last town before Nome.**

❄ **Nulato is the first town north of Kaltag.**

❄ **The Yukon River crosses the route only once. The town closest to the point where the river crosses the route is Whiskey Creek.**

❄ **Ungalik is directly across Norton Bay from Bald Head.**

The dog **Balto** led the team that delivered the serum to Nome on February 2, 1925. He was a symbol of all the heroes who had made the delivery possible through blizzards and temperatures colder than 40° F below zero.

Minto

Nulato

Nine Mile Cabin

Whiskey Creek

Unalakleet

Ungalik

Port Safety

The Great Race of Mercy

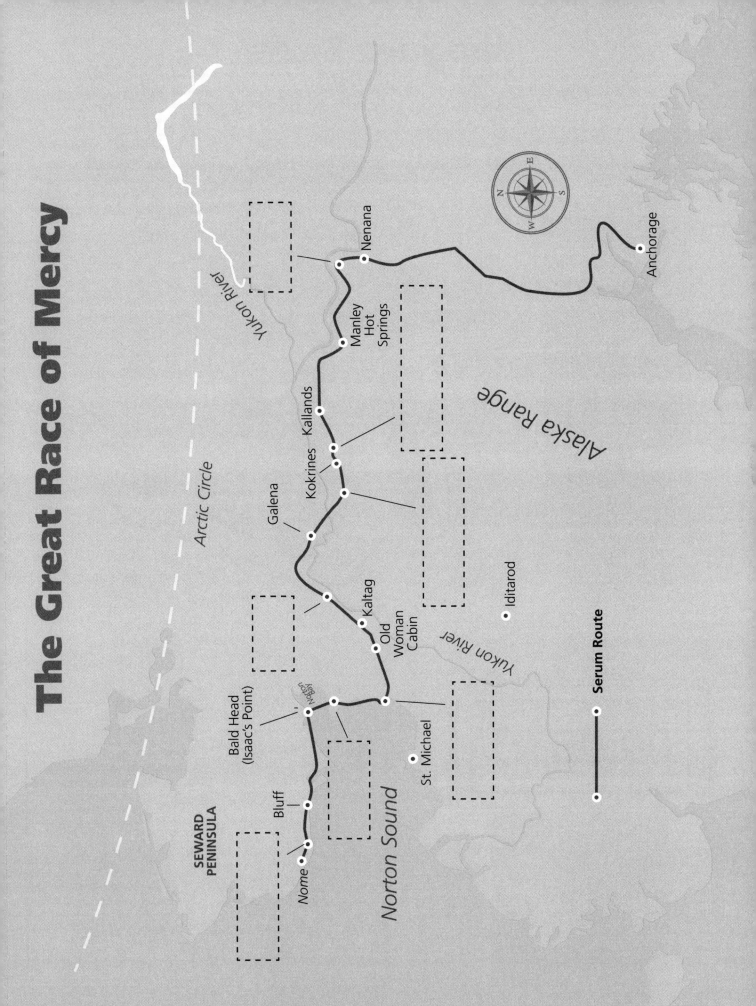

Anchorage

Nenana

Manley Hot Springs

Kallands

Kokrines

Galena

Kaltag

Old Woman Cabin

Bald Head (Isaac's Point)

Bluff

Nome

St. Michael

Iditarod

Yukon River

Yukon River

Alaska Range

Arctic Circle

SEWARD PENINSULA

Norton Sound

Norton Bay

Serum Route

Niagara Falls

Three giant waterfalls fed by the Great Lakes straddle the border of Canada and the United States. Together, they are known as Niagara Falls. Thirty million people visit each year.

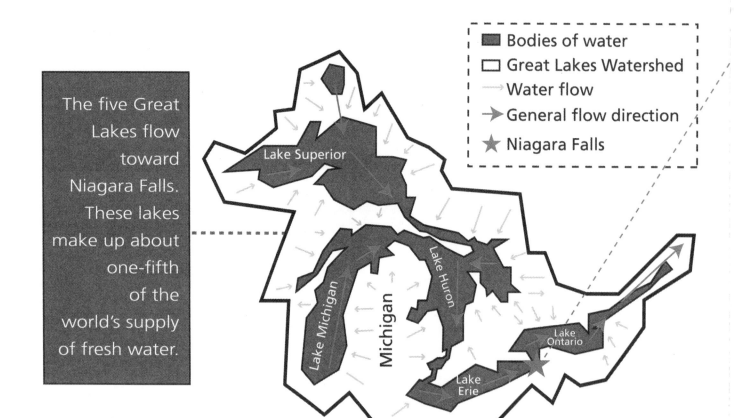

The five Great Lakes flow toward Niagara Falls. These lakes make up about one-fifth of the world's supply of fresh water.

Legend:
- ■ Bodies of water
- □ Great Lakes Watershed
- → Water flow
- ➤ General flow direction
- ★ Niagara Falls

Lake Superior
Lake Michigan
Lake Huron
Michigan
Lake Ontario
Lake Erie

00:00:01

During peak flow, more than 700,000 gallons of water pour over the falls each second.

Daredevils of the Falls

Going over Niagara Falls is illegal and extremely dangerous, but that hasn't stopped people from trying.

1901 – School teacher Annie Taylor rode over the falls in a wooden barrel.

1928 – Jean Lussier made the trip in a large rubber ball.

1985 – Steve Trotter conquered the falls inside a barrel wrapped with inner tubes.

2012 – Tightrope walker Nik Wallenda crossed the falls on a 1,800-foot journey.

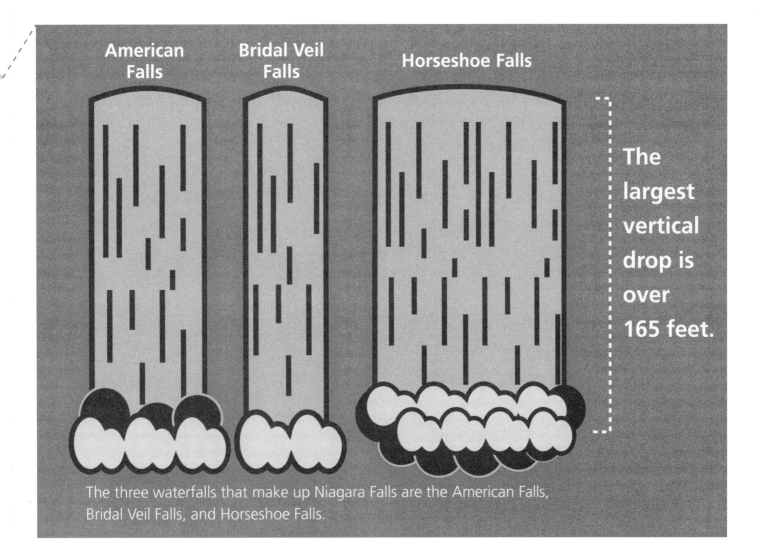

American Falls

Bridal Veil Falls

Horseshoe Falls

The largest vertical drop is over 165 feet.

The three waterfalls that make up Niagara Falls are the American Falls, Bridal Veil Falls, and Horseshoe Falls.

25%

Hydroelectric power is electricity made using the power of moving water. A hydroelectric dam on a river blocks the flowing water. Inside the dam, the tremendous force of the water pushing through it is used to create electricity. Most of the year, 50–75% of the water flowing in the Niagara River above the falls is diverted to hydroelectric power-generating stations. These stations supply at least 25% of the power used in New York state and Ontario, Canada.

Read About It:
HYDROELECTRIC POWER

ONE OF THE FIRST HYDROELECTRIC POWER STATIONS was built on Goat Island at Niagara Falls in the late 1800s. For years, people had looked at the powerful, roaring falls and wondered how all that energy could be put to use. George Westinghouse, the owner of Westinghouse Electric, knew that moving water could be used to generate, or create, electricity. But what was the best way to do it at Niagara Falls? He turned to one of the world's most famous inventors of the time, Nikola Tesla. Tesla designed a power station that used the weight of falling water to make electricity. In 1896, the Niagara Falls Power Plant was up and running on Goat Island, which is located between Bridal Veil and Horseshoe Falls. Within a few years, the plant was creating enough electricity to light up New York City.

Nikola Tesla

So how can water create electricity? The water itself does not create the electricity. A hydroelectric power plant uses the weight and movement of falling water to make electricity. A river full of flowing water is a very powerful force. A hydroelectric power plant, such as a dam, sends the water down through a tunnel. Inside the tunnel, there is a giant wheel, called a *turbine*. The tremendous force of the water falling down through the tunnel spins the turbine. The turbine is attached to an electrical generator, which is a machine that makes electricity. Inside the generator, metal wires and magnets spin to create electricity. The electricity that is generated then flows through wires all the way to wherever electricity is needed.

Think and Solve

Study the infographic and read the passage on page 20. Answer the questions.

1. Who designed the Niagara Falls Power Plant?

_____

2. Goat Island is located between _____ and _____.

3. Where does the water come from that feeds Niagara Falls?

    A. from the Atlantic Ocean

    B. from Hudson Bay

    C. from the Great Lakes

    D. from the Pacific Ocean

4. During peak flow, about how much water pours over the falls in one minute?

    A. 420,000 gallons

    B. 700,000 gallons

    C. 42,000,000 gallons

    D. 700,000,000 gallons

5. About how many people visit Niagara Falls each year?

_____

6. Number the steps 1–5 to show the order used to create hydroelectric power.

_____ The turbine spins an electric generator.

_____ Swiftly moving water flows into a tunnel.

_____ Electricity flows through wires to power buildings and machines.

_____The force of the water turns a turbine.

_____The generator uses wires and magnets to create electricity.

7. Use what you know about hydroelectricity to describe how a windmill is used to create electricity.

_____

_____

_____

I Have a Dream

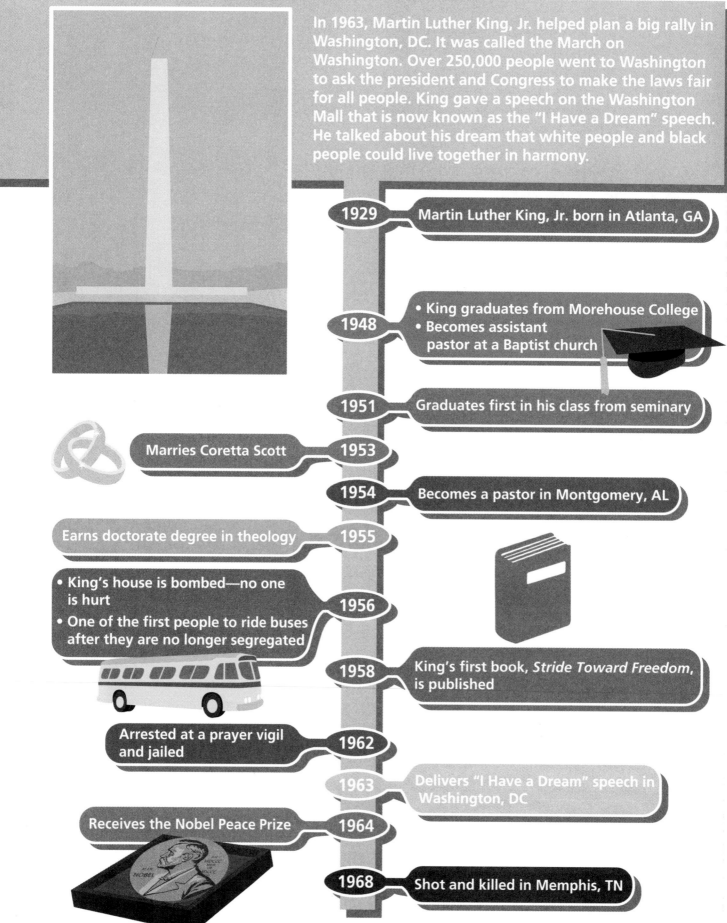

In 1963, Martin Luther King, Jr. helped plan a big rally in Washington, DC. It was called the March on Washington. Over 250,000 people went to Washington to ask the president and Congress to make the laws fair for all people. King gave a speech on the Washington Mall that is now known as the "I Have a Dream" speech. He talked about his dream that white people and black people could live together in harmony.

1929 Martin Luther King, Jr. born in Atlanta, GA

1948
- King graduates from Morehouse College
- Becomes assistant pastor at a Baptist church

1951 Graduates first in his class from seminary

Marries Coretta Scott **1953**

1954 Becomes a pastor in Montgomery, AL

Earns doctorate degree in theology **1955**

- King's house is bombed—no one is hurt
- One of the first people to ride buses after they are no longer segregated **1956**

1958 King's first book, *Stride Toward Freedom*, is published

Arrested at a prayer vigil and jailed **1962**

1963 Delivers "I Have a Dream" speech in Washington, DC

Receives the Nobel Peace Prize **1964**

1968 Shot and killed in Memphis, TN

Think and Solve
Study the infographic. Answer the questions.

1. How old was Martin Luther King, Jr. when his first book was published?

_____

2. True or false? King received the Pulitzer Prize in Politics.

_____

3. Martin Luther King, Jr. was married in _____.

4. In which city was King assassinated?

    A. Memphis, Tennessee   **C.** Atlanta, Georgia

    B. Washington, DC   **D.** Montgomery, Alabama

5. In what city did King give his "I Have a Dream" speech? _____

Make a Time Line
Who is your hero? If it is someone you know, interview him or her. If it is someone famous, research his or her life using a resource such as an encyclopedia, an approved Internet source, or a biography. Use the time line below to record six important dates and events from your hero's life.

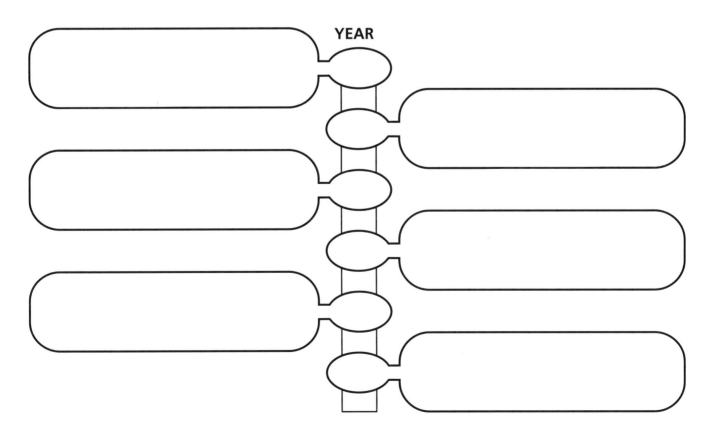

YEAR

Graveyard of the Atlantic

Since the 1500s, more than 3,000 ships have wrecked off the coast of North Carolina. Hurricanes, underwater sandbars, shoals, and strong currents combine to make this region of the Atlantic Ocean treacherous for sailors. Today, scuba divers can explore this region to scout out the wrecks of pirate ships, colonial trade vessels, battleships, and more.

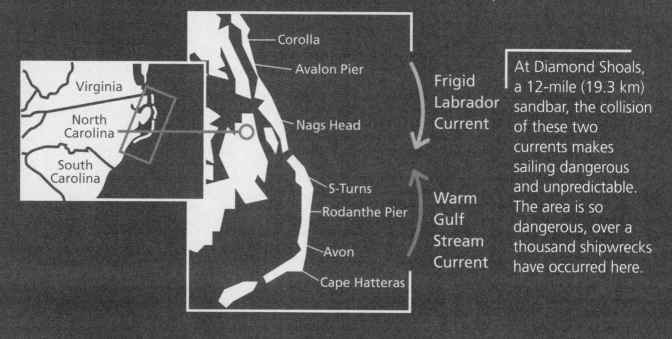

Corolla
Avalon Pier
Nags Head
S-Turns
Rodanthe Pier
Avon
Cape Hatteras

Virginia
North Carolina
South Carolina

Frigid Labrador Current

Warm Gulf Stream Current

At Diamond Shoals, a 12-mile (19.3 km) sandbar, the collision of these two currents makes sailing dangerous and unpredictable. The area is so dangerous, over a thousand shipwrecks have occurred here.

Shipwrecks Through the Centuries

USS *Monitor* • 171 feet (52 m)
• Sank 1862

USS *Atlanta* • 204 feet (62 m)
• Sank 1869

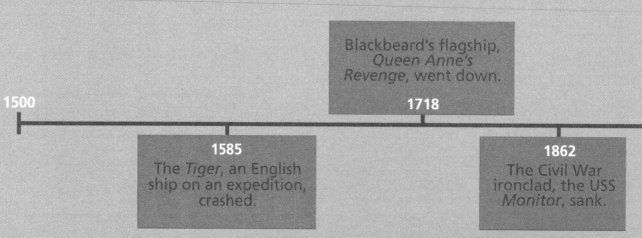

Blackbeard's flagship, *Queen Anne's Revenge*, went down.

1500

1718

1585
The *Tiger*, an English ship on an expedition, crashed.

1862
The Civil War ironclad, the USS *Monitor*, sank.

Pirates of the Atlantic

From 1716 to 1718, Blackbeard was the most feared pirate in the Atlantic. Some ships surrendered without a fight when Blackbeard and his crew came aboard.

The pirate Bartholomew Roberts, or "Black Bart," captured more than 400 ships during the four years he sailed the seas. In 1722, he and his crew took over a fleet of 11 ships!

Calico Jack also terrorized the seas during Blackbeard's time. Jack was famous for including women in his crew.

Captain Morgan attacked Spanish ships. England and Spain were at war, so King Charles II of England liked Morgan. In fact, the king made Morgan a knight in 1674!

USS _Schurz_ • 275 feet (84 m)
• Sank 1918

Proteus • 390 feet (119 m)
• Sank 1918

U-352 • 115 feet (35 m)
• Sank 1942

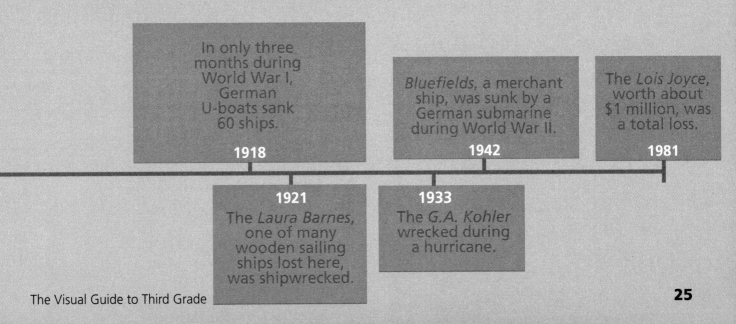

In only three months during World War I, German U-boats sank 60 ships.

1918

Bluefields, a merchant ship, was sunk by a German submarine during World War II.

1942

The _Lois Joyce_, worth about $1 million, was a total loss.

1981

1921
The _Laura Barnes_, one of many wooden sailing ships lost here, was shipwrecked.

1933
The _G.A. Kohler_ wrecked during a hurricane.

Think and Solve

Study the infographic. Answer the questions.

1. Where is the Graveyard of the Atlantic?

    A. off the coast of South Carolina

    B. off the coast of North Carolina

    C. off the coast of Virginia

    D. all of the above

2. Diamond Shoals is a _____.

    A. coral reef

    B. famous shipwreck

    C. sandbar

    D. city

3. How many feet longer was the *Proteus* than the USS *Atlanta*?

    _____

4. Which boat sank in 1862?

    _____

5. Blackbeard, Black Bart, and Calico Jack were all part of the same crew.

    True   False

6. What shipwreck occurred in 1718?

    _____

7. During which war did German U-boats sink 60 ships?

    _____

8. Nags Head is north of Corolla.

    True   False

9. Why does the time line go back only as far as the year 1500?

    _____

10. Why is the area near the coast nicknamed "The Graveyard of the Atlantic"?

    _____

    _____

Piece It Together

Blackbeard's ship, the *Queen Anne's Revenge*, was a large *frigate*, or warship. The words on the labels below describe different parts of a similar ship. Read each definition. Then, cut out the labels and glue or tape them on the diagram on page 29.

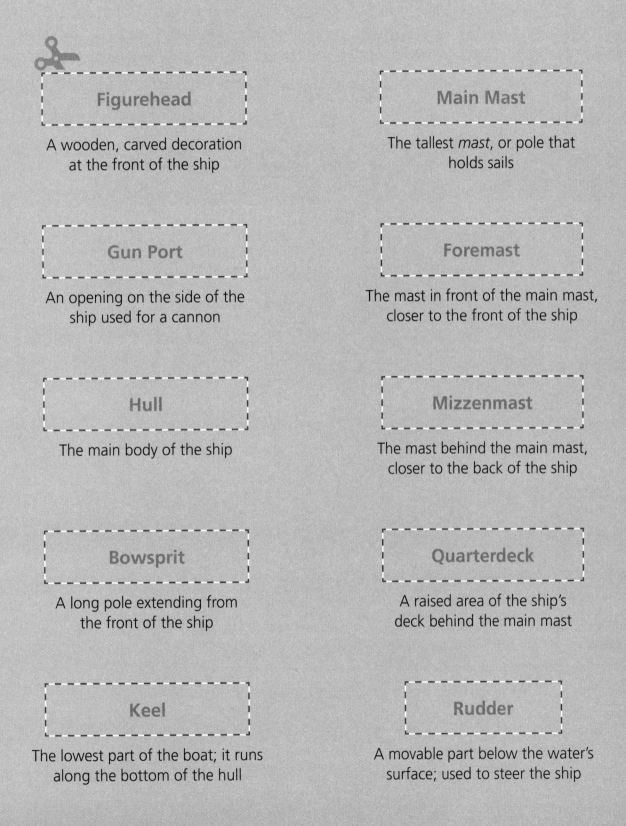

Figurehead

A wooden, carved decoration at the front of the ship

Main Mast

The tallest *mast*, or pole that holds sails

Gun Port

An opening on the side of the ship used for a cannon

Foremast

The mast in front of the main mast, closer to the front of the ship

Hull

The main body of the ship

Mizzenmast

The mast behind the main mast, closer to the back of the ship

Bowsprit

A long pole extending from the front of the ship

Quarterdeck

A raised area of the ship's deck behind the main mast

Keel

The lowest part of the boat; it runs along the bottom of the hull

Rudder

A movable part below the water's surface; used to steer the ship

A Pirate Ship

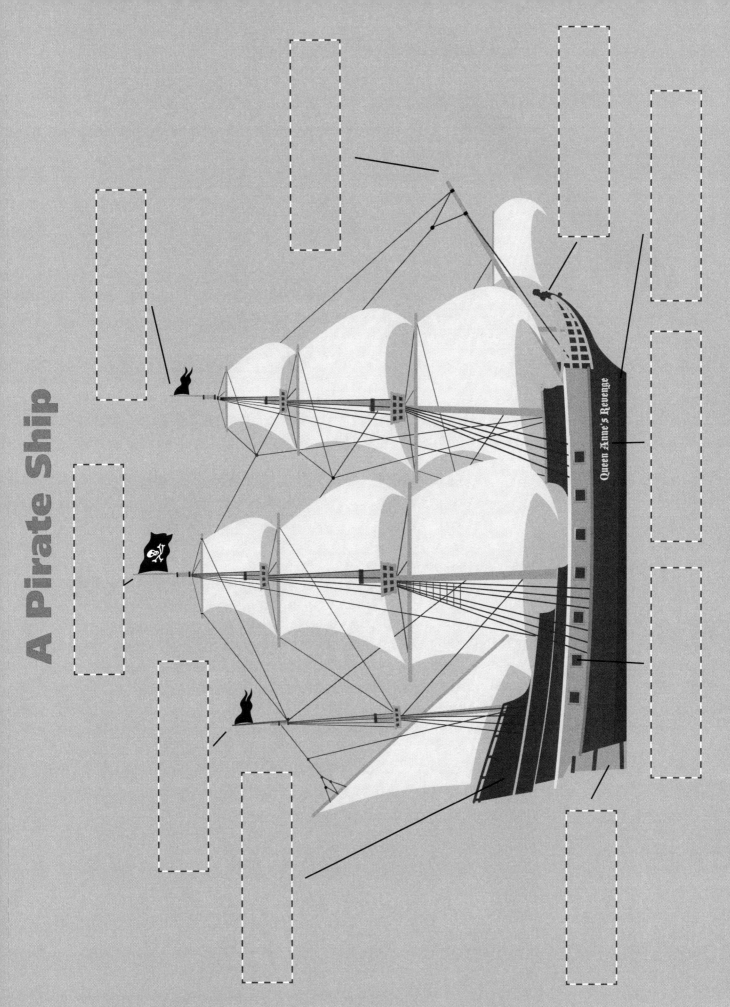

Queen Anne's Revenge

One of a Kind

The ridges on our fingertips make fingerprints. They are completely unique. No two people have the same fingerprints!

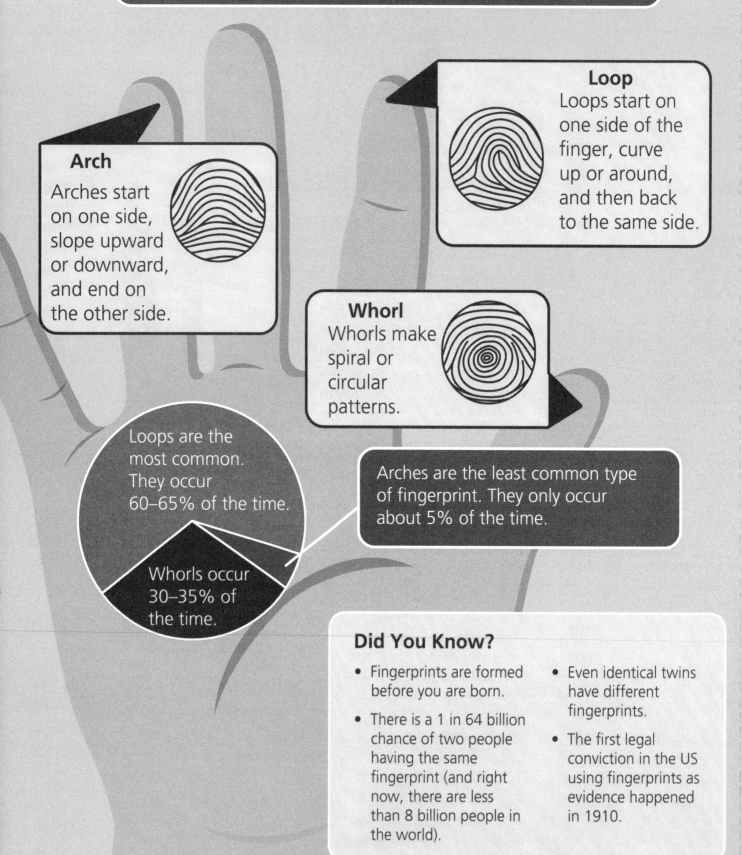

Arch
Arches start on one side, slope upward or downward, and end on the other side.

Loop
Loops start on one side of the finger, curve up or around, and then back to the same side.

Whorl
Whorls make spiral or circular patterns.

Loops are the most common. They occur 60–65% of the time.

Whorls occur 30–35% of the time.

Arches are the least common type of fingerprint. They only occur about 5% of the time.

Did You Know?

- Fingerprints are formed before you are born.

- There is a 1 in 64 billion chance of two people having the same fingerprint (and right now, there are less than 8 billion people in the world).

- Even identical twins have different fingerprints.

- The first legal conviction in the US using fingerprints as evidence happened in 1910.

Try It Yourself
Making your own ink pad for taking fingerprints is easy.

1. Mix together equal amounts of water and kids' washable paint. Stir well.

2. Cut a dry sponge in half and place it in the paint mixture. Allow it to soak up the paint for about 30 seconds.

3. Squeeze out the extra paint into the sink. The sponge should be damp but not soaking.

4. Place the sponge in a small dish.

5. Gently press your finger into the sponge to coat it in the paint/water mixture.

6. To make a fingerprint, roll your finger from one side to the other on a sheet of paper.

Use your ink pad to make a print of each of your fingers in the spaces below. Use the infographic to help you identify the patterns you see.

Right Hand

FINGER	Thumb	Index Finger	Middle Finger	Ring Finger	Pinky Finger
PRINT					
PATTERN					

Left Hand

FINGER	Thumb	Index Finger	Middle Finger	Ring Finger	Pinky Finger
PRINT					
PATTERN					

State Nicknames

Did you know that each US state has a nickname?

Washington The Evergreen State

Oregon The Beaver State

Idaho The Gem State

Montana The Treasure State

North Dakota The Peace Garden State

Minnesota The North Star State

South Dakota The Mount Rushmore State

Wyoming The Equality State

Nebraska The Cornhusker State

Iowa The Hawkeye State

Nevada The Silver State

Utah The Beehive State

Colorado The Centennial State

Kansas The Sunflower State

Missouri The Show Me State

California The Golden State

Arizona The Grand Canyon State

New Mexico The Land of Enchantment

Oklahoma The Sooner State

Arkansas The Natural State

Texas The Lone Star State

Alaska The Last Frontier

Hawaii The Aloha State

Louisiana The Pelican State

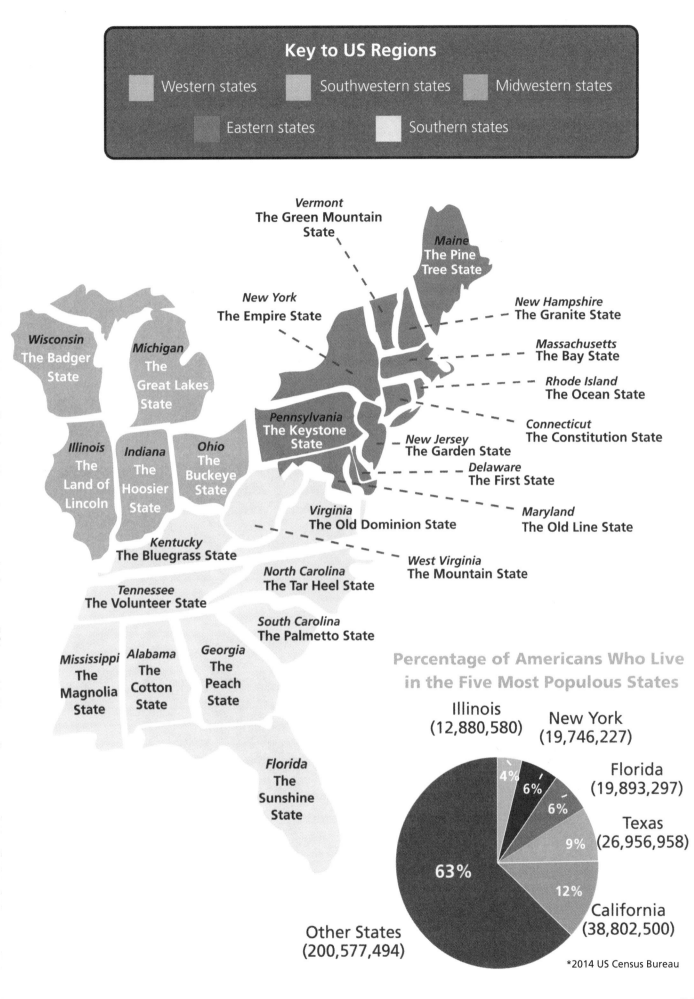

Key to US Regions

- Western states
- Southwestern states
- Midwestern states
- Eastern states
- Southern states

Vermont
The Green Mountain State

Maine
The Pine Tree State

New York
The Empire State

New Hampshire
The Granite State

Wisconsin
The Badger State

Michigan
The Great Lakes State

Massachusetts
The Bay State

Rhode Island
The Ocean State

Pennsylvania
The Keystone State

Connecticut
The Constitution State

Illinois
The Land of Lincoln

Indiana
The Hoosier State

Ohio
The Buckeye State

New Jersey
The Garden State

Delaware
The First State

Virginia
The Old Dominion State

Maryland
The Old Line State

Kentucky
The Bluegrass State

West Virginia
The Mountain State

North Carolina
The Tar Heel State

Tennessee
The Volunteer State

South Carolina
The Palmetto State

Mississippi
The Magnolia State

Alabama
The Cotton State

Georgia
The Peach State

Percentage of Americans Who Live in the Five Most Populous States

Illinois (12,880,580)

New York (19,746,227)

Florida (19,893,297)

Texas (26,956,958)

California (38,802,500)

Florida
The Sunshine State

4%
6%
6%
9%
12%
63%

Other States (200,577,494)

*2014 US Census Bureau

Read About It:
STATE STORIES

HOW DID STATES GET THEIR NICKNAMES? Some are obvious. Delaware is called "The First State" because it was the first state to sign the US Constitution. Rhode Island's nickname, "The Ocean State," makes sense because Rhode Island is right beside the Atlantic Ocean. Other state nicknames have a story behind them. Alaska has several nicknames. One is "Land of the Midnight Sun." Because Alaska is located so far north, for part of the year, the sun never sets completely. It is light 24 hours a day, even at midnight! Alaska is also known as "Seward's Folly." Secretary of State William Seward made the deal to purchase Alaska from Russia in 1867. It was so cold, wild, and isolated that many people thought the purchase was a *folly*, or foolish idea.

Categorize It
Write state nicknames for each category.

1. Write three state nicknames that include animals.

_____   _____   _____

2. Write two state nicknames that include the word *sun*.

_____   _____

3. Write three state nicknames that include bodies of water.

_____   _____   _____

4. Which state is nicknamed after a fruit?

_____

5. Write two state nicknames that include metals.

_____

_____

Alaska

The Last Frontier *or* Land of the Midnight Sun

Spend a few minutes studying the map on pages 32–33.
Then, see how many state names you can fill in on the map below. Answer the questions.

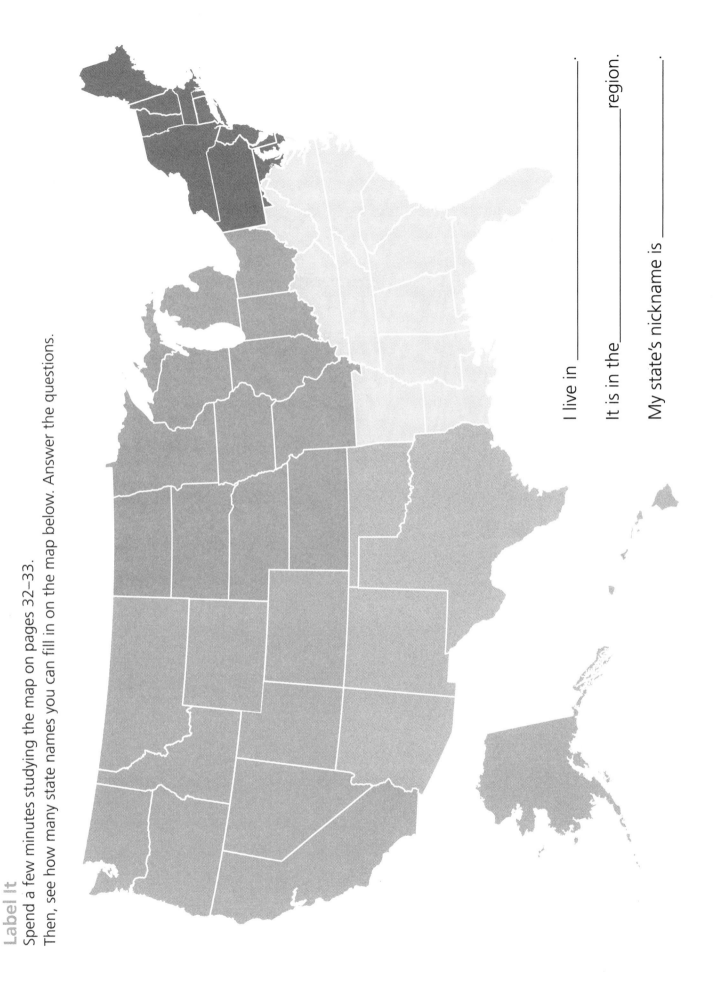

I live in _____ .

It is in the _____ region.

My state's nickname is _____ .

The Nation's Front Yard

The National Mall in Washington, DC, was built for the people. It draws millions of visitors a year from around the world. Visitors walk the long plot of grass stretching from the Washington Monument to the US Capitol. They gather there for speeches, Fourth of July fireworks, and other events. Some of the world's finest museums line the streets beside the Mall.

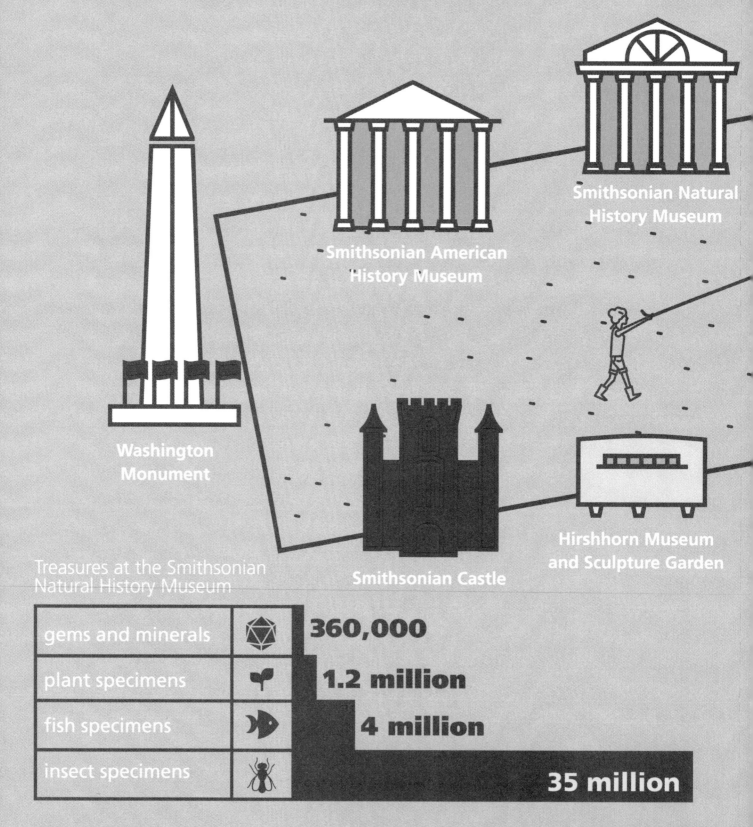

Smithsonian Natural History Museum

Smithsonian American History Museum

Washington Monument

Smithsonian Castle

Hirshhorn Museum and Sculpture Garden

Treasures at the Smithsonian Natural History Museum

gems and minerals	🔶	360,000
plant specimens	🌱	1.2 million
fish specimens	🐟	4 million
insect specimens	🐜	35 million

National Gallery of Art

National Gallery Sculpture Garden

Ulysses S. Grant Memorial

US Capitol

Capitol Reflecting Pool

Smithsonian American Indian Museum

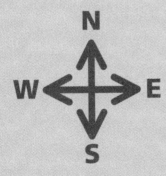

Smithsonian Air and Space Museum

N
W   E
S

The National Stage

Throughout history, the National Mall has been the site of important events.

1814—During the War of 1812, British troops attacked Washington, DC. They burned several buildings, including the Capitol Building and the White House.

1848—Thousands of people attended the ceremony marking the start of construction of the Washington Monument.

1913—Thousands of women marched from the Capitol Building toward the White House demanding the right to vote.

1937—25,000 scouts attended the first Boy Scout Jamboree on the Mall. They set up camp around the Washington Monument and were visited by President Franklin D. Roosevelt.

1963—250,000 people heard Martin Luther King, Jr. give his "I Have a Dream" speech during the March on Washington for Jobs and Freedom.

Think and Solve

Study the infographic. Answer the questions.

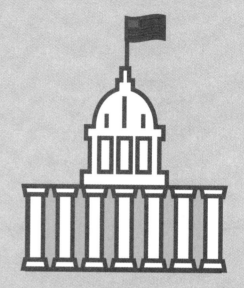

1. There are more than 30 million plant specimens at the Museum of Natural History.

   True   **False**

2. Which direction would you walk to go from the National Gallery of Art to the Smithsonian Air and Space Museum?

   A. north and west

   B. east and south

   C. south and west

   D. west and north

3. Which museum would you visit if you wanted to learn more about astronauts?

   _____

4. The National Gallery Sculpture Garden is inside the National Gallery of Art.

   True   **False**

5. In what year did construction begin on the Washington Monument?

   _____

Schedule It

Plan a day of sightseeing along the National Mall. Keep in mind that each museum has many things to look at. You will not be able to see everything in one day! Choose which places you most want to visit and how long you will spend at each one. Don't forget to include time for lunch! Write your plan on the schedule below.

8:00 A.M. _____	**2:00 P.M.** _____
9:00 A.M. _____	**3:00 P.M.** _____
10:00 A.M. _____	**4:00 P.M.** _____
11:00 A.M. _____	**5:00 P.M.** _____
12:00 P.M. _____	**6:00 P.M.** _____
1:00 P.M. _____	**7:00 P.M.** _____

Map It

Use the key below to draw a map of your neighborhood. Be sure to label the names of roads, buildings, and other important locations.

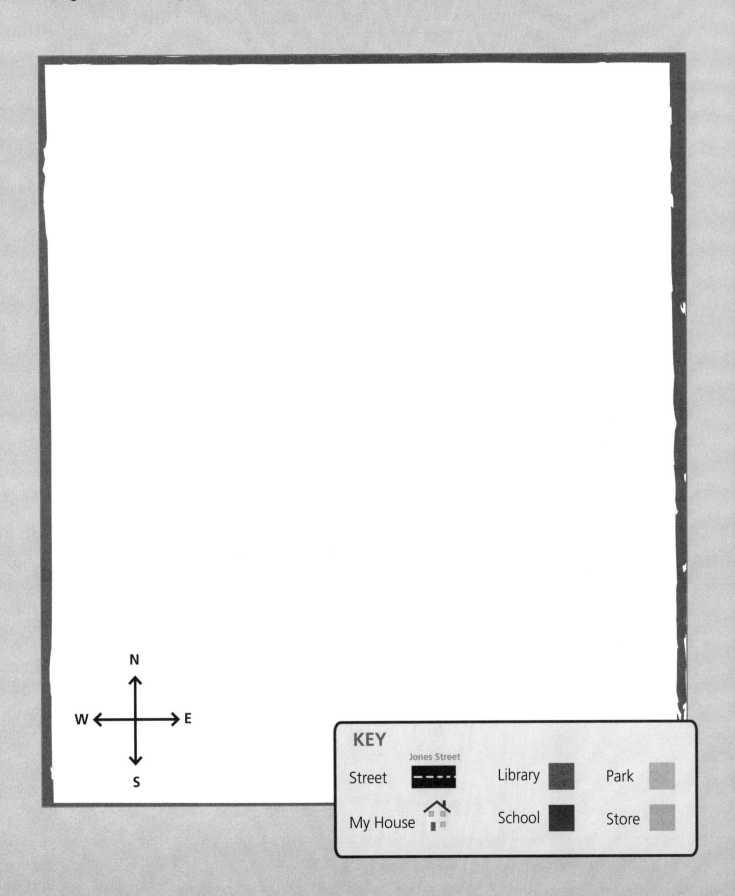

N

W ← → E

S

KEY

Street — Jones Street

My House 🏠

Library ■

School ■

Park ■

Store ■

Pictures in the Sky

A *constellation* is a group of stars that forms a pattern in the sky. Constellations may look like animals, people, objects, or figures from mythology. The stars aren't actually related to each other. They just appear to make a pattern when viewed from Earth.

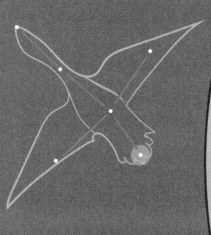

Cygnus
The Swan

★ It is also known as the Northern Cross.

★ Its brightest star, Deneb, is 1,500 light-years from Earth.

★ It can be seen in the northern sky.

Cassiopeia
The Queen

★ Its brightest star, Schedar, is 40 times larger than the diameter of the Sun.

★ Its brightest stars make a W shape.

★ It can be seen in the northeastern sky.

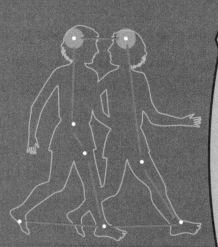

Gemini
The Twins

★ Gemini's two brightest stars are Castor and Pollux.

★ In Greek mythology, Castor and Pollux are sons of the god Zeus.

★ Winter and spring are good times to look for Gemini in the night sky.

Leo
The Lion

★ Looking for a backward question mark can help you identify Leo.

★ Blue-white Regulus is Leo's brightest star.

★ Leo is easiest to spot on spring evenings.

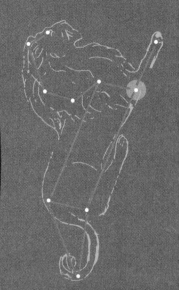

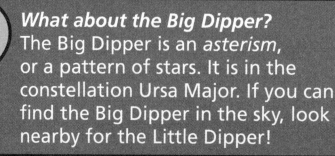

? ***What about the Big Dipper?***
The Big Dipper is an *asterism*, or a pattern of stars. It is in the constellation Ursa Major. If you can find the Big Dipper in the sky, look nearby for the Little Dipper!

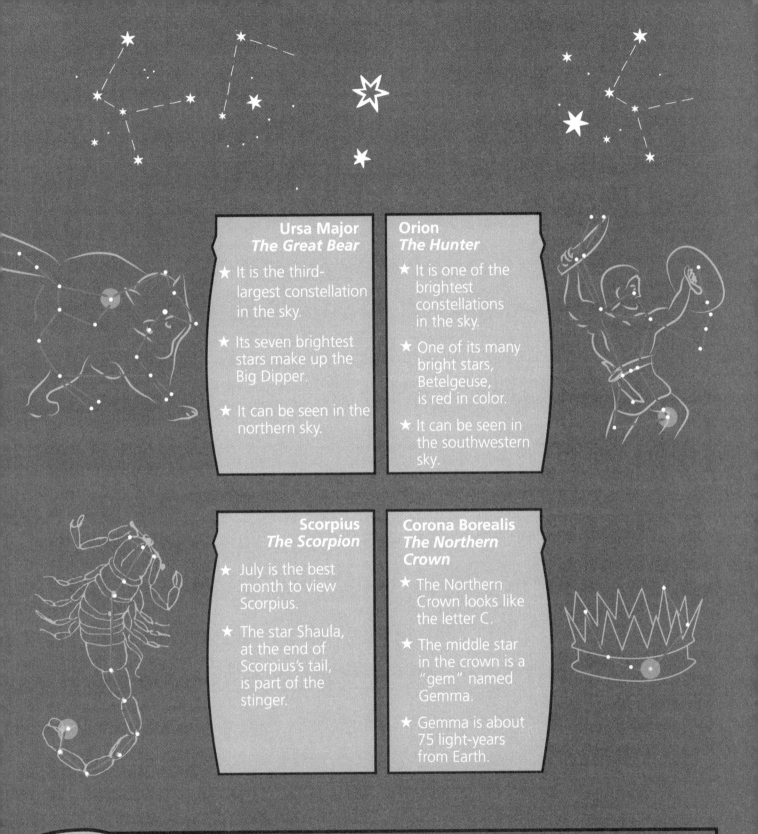

Ursa Major
The Great Bear

★ It is the third-largest constellation in the sky.

★ Its seven brightest stars make up the Big Dipper.

★ It can be seen in the northern sky.

Orion
The Hunter

★ It is one of the brightest constellations in the sky.

★ One of its many bright stars, Betelgeuse, is red in color.

★ It can be seen in the southwestern sky.

Scorpius
The Scorpion

★ July is the best month to view Scorpius.

★ The star Shaula, at the end of Scorpius's tail, is part of the stinger.

Corona Borealis
The Northern Crown

★ The Northern Crown looks like the letter C.

★ The middle star in the crown is a "gem" named Gemma.

★ Gemma is about 75 light-years from Earth.

How close are the stars in a constellation? Check out how far apart the main stars in Orion are from Earth.

OUR VIEW

SIDE VIEW

Earth

0   25   50   75   100   125   150   175   200   225

LIGHT-YEARS

Read About It:
COYOTE AND THE BEARS

Like many other ancient groups, Native Americans created constellation myths. The following story is from the Wasco Tribe of Oregon. It tells the story of the constellation we know as the Big Dipper.

ONE NIGHT, FIVE WOLVES STARED UP AT THE SKY. Coyote came upon them and asked what they were looking at.

"There are two animals up there, but we have no way to reach them," they replied.

Coyote thought for a moment and then took out his bow. He shot an arrow into the sky, and then shot another, which stuck into the first. He continued to shoot until a chain of arrows reached the ground. The five wolves and Coyote climbed the ladder into the sky, along with a dog that followed one of the wolves. When they reached the sky, they discovered that the animals they had seen were grizzly bears. The wolves sat near the bears and stared, and the bears stared right back at them. Coyote liked the way they looked, so he climbed back down his arrow ladder and left them all there.

The wolves make up the handle and bowl of the Big Dipper. The bears are the two stars on the front of the bowl. The small star by the wolf in the center of the handle is the dog.

Try It Yourself
Connect the stars below to form a new constellation. Name your constellation. Then, write a short story about it on the lines.

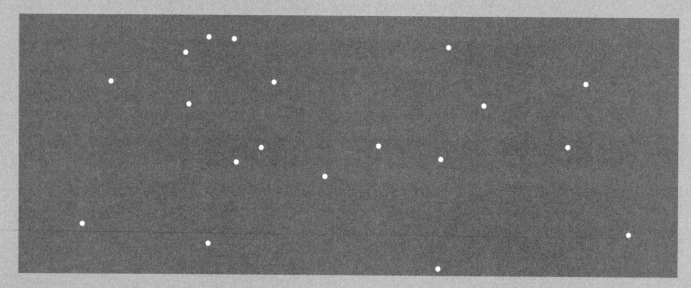

Constellation Name: _____

Constellation Story: _____

_____

_____

_____

Explore Your World

Go outside with an adult on four different clear nights. Can you observe the moon, stars, planets, or constellations? Draw what you see in the spaces below. Try to write the name of each celestial object you see. If you need help, refer to a star-gazing guide you find at the library or online.

I saw: _____.

I saw: _____.

I saw: _____.

I saw: _____.

World's Longest Rivers

Nile — The Nile River flows through 10 countries.

Amazon — There are more than 3,000 different kinds of fish living in the Amazon River.

Yangtze

Yellow

Paraná

Congo — People living by the Congo River use its water to irrigate their peanut, sugarcane, cotton, and tobacco crops.

Lena

Mekong — The Mekong River has many other names, such as River of Stone and Dragon Running River.

Irtysh

Niger

Mississippi

0   500   1,000   1,500   2,000

Rivers are an important part of human life. They provide water, food, and transportation. Most major world cities are located near the banks of rivers. The length of a river is measured from its source to its mouth. The *source* is where the river begins. The *mouth* is where the river flows into a larger body of water, such as the ocean.

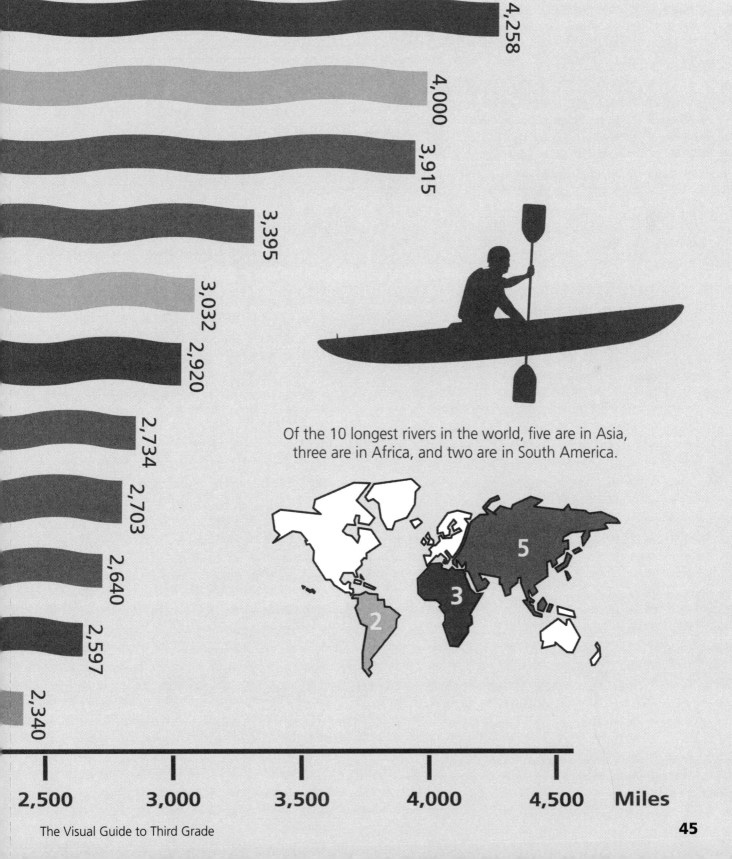

4,258

4,000

3,915

3,395

3,032

2,920

2,734

2,703

2,640

2,597

2,340

Of the 10 longest rivers in the world, five are in Asia, three are in Africa, and two are in South America.

5

3

2

2,500   3,000   3,500   4,000   4,500   **Miles**

Do the Math
Study the infographic. Solve the problems.

1. The Amazon River and the Paraná River are in South America. How many combined miles of the longest rivers run through South America?

_____

2. How much longer is the Nile than the Mekong River?

_____

3. True or false? The Nile is more than twice as long as the Mississippi River.

_____

4. How far is it from the source of the Niger River to the mouth of the Niger River?

_____

5. True or false? The infographic shows the lengths of 10 rivers.

_____

Explore Your World
Ask an adult to take you to a river near your home. Sit quietly and observe the area for several minutes. Draw the river in the box below. Then, use the lines to record your observations.

What I Saw: _____

_____

What I Heard: _____

_____

What I Smelled: _____

_____

What I Felt: _____

_____

Research and Report
Use a reliable resource to research the longest rivers in your state.
Use the chart below to record what you find.

	Name of River	Length in Miles
River 1		
River 2		
River 3		
River 4		
River 5		

Now, use the information from your chart to make a graph comparing the rivers.
Your graph should look similar to the one on pages 44 and 45.

Rivers

_____

_____

_____

_____

_____

Length in Miles

Sleep From A to Zzz

Sleepy Sayings

Catch 40 winks

Sleep on it

Sleep like a log

Hit the hay

Take a cat nap

Get some shut-eye

Hours of Sleep Each Day

Sleep is important! Doctors recommend different amounts of sleep for different ages. How do you match up?

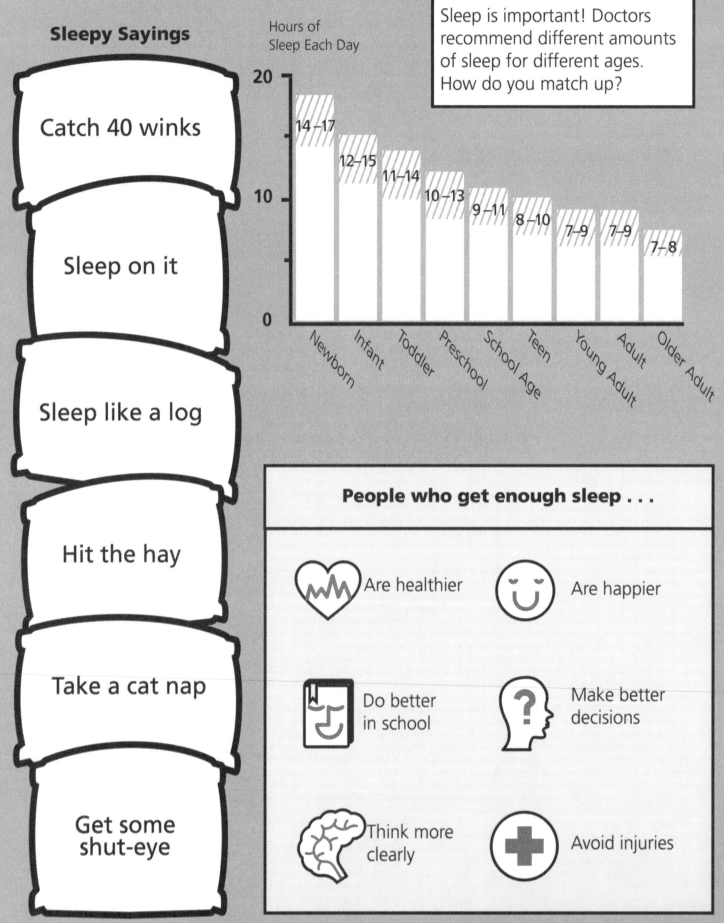

Newborn 14–17
Infant 12–15
Toddler 11–14
Preschool 10–13
School Age 9–11
Teen 8–10
Young Adult 7–9
Adult 7–9
Older Adult 7–8

People who get enough sleep . . .

Are healthier

Are happier

Do better in school

Make better decisions

Think more clearly

Avoid injuries

What Happens When You Sleep?

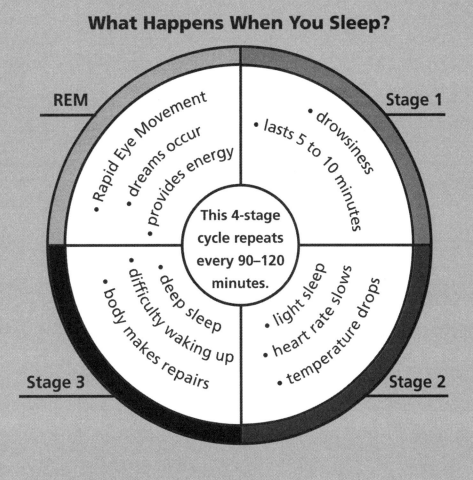

REM
- Rapid Eye Movement
- dreams occur
- provides energy

Stage 1
- drowsiness
- lasts 5 to 10 minutes

This 4-stage cycle repeats every 90–120 minutes.

Stage 3
- deep sleep
- difficulty waking up
- body makes repairs

Stage 2
- light sleep
- heart rate slows
- temperature drops

How to get a good night's sleep . . .

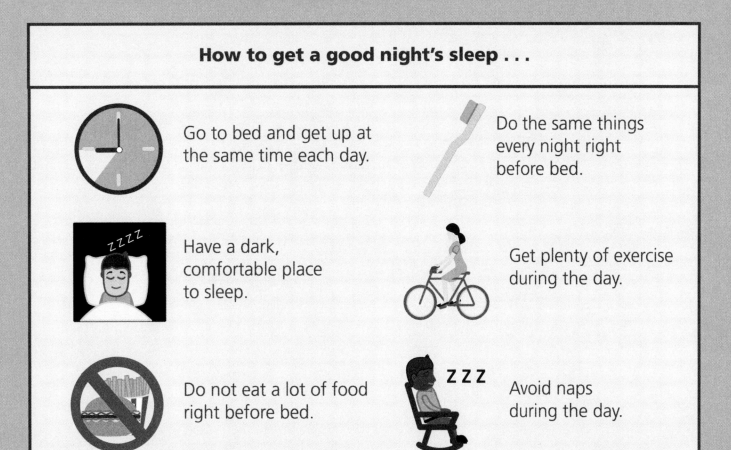

Go to bed and get up at the same time each day.

Do the same things every night right before bed.

Have a dark, comfortable place to sleep.

Get plenty of exercise during the day.

Do not eat a lot of food right before bed.

Avoid naps during the day.

Log It

Keep a sleep log for five nights. Use the chart below to record the number of hours you sleep each night.

	Time you went to bed	Time you woke up	Total hours of sleep
Night 1			
Night 2			
Night 3			
Night 4			
Night 5			

Make a Bar Graph

Use the information from your chart to make a bar graph showing the number of hours you slept each night. Start at the bottom. Color one space for each hour you slept each night.

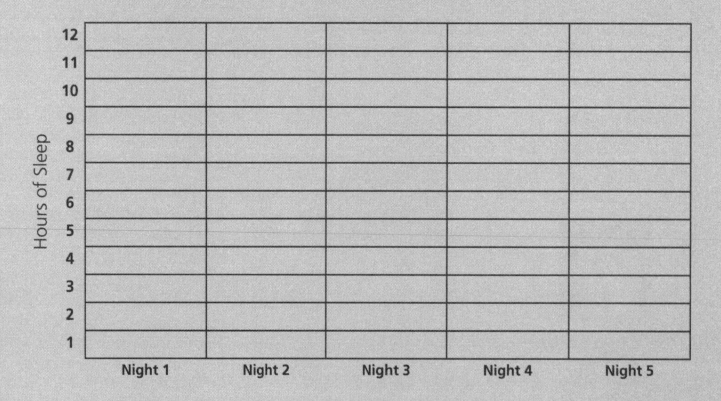

Hours of Sleep

12
11
10
9
8
7
6
5
4
3
2
1

Night 1   Night 2   Night 3   Night 4   Night 5

Show It

On the clock below, color in the hours when you are usually asleep.

Write About It

Dreams can be interesting, fun, weird, or even scary. What happens in your dreams?
On the lines below, describe a dream you remember.

_____

_____

_____

_____

_____

_____

_____

_____

_____

_____

Vitamins and Minerals

A 600 mcg daily*
- improves vision
- boosts the immune system
- helps cells grow

B₆ 1.0 mg daily
- keeps the brain healthy
- fights various diseases
- helps to digest protein

B₁₂ 1.8 mcg daily
- boosts the mood
- increases energy
- helps with concentration

C 45 mg daily
- protects the eyes
- keeps the heart healthy
- boosts the immune system

D 15 mcg daily
- strengthens the bones
- reduces the risk of diabetes
- regulates the immune system

E 11 mg daily
- boosts the immune system
- promotes healthy skin
- benefits the eyes

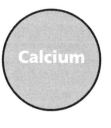

Calcium 1,300 mg daily
- strengthens the bones
- maintains healthy heart rhythm
- builds muscle strength

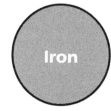

Iron 8 mg daily
- transports oxygen through the body
- increases energy
- promotes healthy skin, hair, and nails

Potassium 4,500 mg daily
- helps to prevent heart disease
- promotes kidney health
- prevents digestive disorders

Sodium 2,200 mg daily
- maintains body fluids
- improves muscle health
- regulates blood pressure

*Recommendations are for 9–12-year-old males and females and are based on the USDA Dietary Guidelines for Americans, 2010.

Peanut Butter

1 tbsp.	7 mg	11% Vitamin E*
	125 mg	1% Calcium
	57 mg	3% Potassium
	2 mg	2% Sodium

Pizza

1 slice (of 8)	0.1 mg	8% B₆
	155 mg	16% Calcium
	2 mg	10% Iron
	469 mg	20% Sodium

Broccoli

1 cup	101 mg	134% Vitamin C
	62 mg	6% Calcium
	1 mg	6% Iron
	454 mg	10% Potassium

Blueberries

1 cup	14 mg	19% Vitamin C
	1 mg	6% Vitamin E
	9 mg	1% Calcium
	114 mg	2% Potassium

*Daily values shown for an average adult.

The Visual Guide to Third Grade

Research and Report

How nutritious is the food in your cupboard? Choose a food product from home and look for the nutrition label on the packaging. Use the information from the label to fill in the blank label.

Name of Food Product:

_____

Nutrition Facts

Serving Size
Servings per Container

Amount Per Serving	
Calories	Calories from Fat
	% Daily Value
Total Fat	
Saturated Fat	
Cholesterol	
Sodium	
Total Carbohydrate	
Dietary Fiber	
Sugars	
Protein	
Vitamin	

* Percent Daily Values are based on a 2,000 calorie diet.

Make a Chart

Do the foods you eat each day contain the RDA (Recommended Daily Allowance) of vitamins and minerals? Choose a vitamin or mineral listed on page 52. Using the chart below, keep track of the foods you eat during one day. For each food, record the percent of your daily need it provided of the vitamin or mineral you chose. To find the percentage, read the label for each food or ask an adult to help you research it online. Then, color in the pie chart to show the total percentage you received for the day.

Vitamin or mineral: _____

Food	% of RDA
Total:	

Total % of your daily requirement for the vitamin/mineral

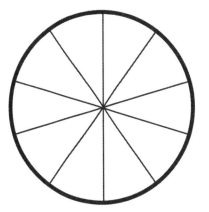

(Hint: The pie chart is divided into sections showing 10% each.)

Giant Squid

A giant squid is huge—the second-largest living invertebrate! An *invertebrate* has no spine.

They have eight arms with two-inch (5 cm) toothed suckers on the undersides.

The two long feeding tentacles are weapons, with hundreds of sharp-toothed suckers on the ends. Squid can snatch prey from 33 feet (10 m) away. They like to eat shrimp, fish, and other squid.

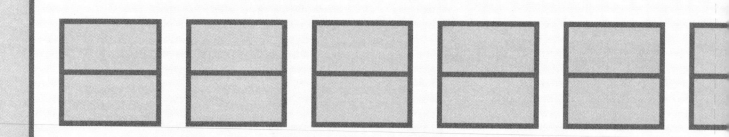

On average, giant squid are about 45 feet (13 m) long. That is just about as long as an ordinary school bus.

The largest giant squid ever found weighed nearly a ton (900 kg). That's about as heavy as a full-grown polar bear!

Their eyes are enormous, about as large as dinner plates.

10 in.

Giant squid are a mystery. They are rarely seen because they live deep in the ocean. The first live one was photographed in 2006.

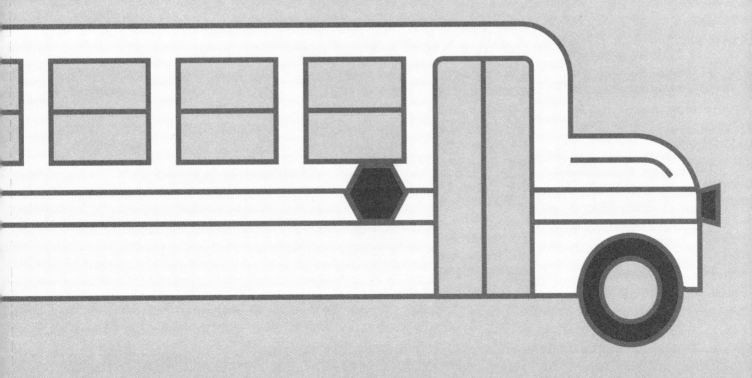

Think and Solve

Study the infographic.
Answer the questions.

1. A vertebrate is an animal that has a spine. What is an animal called that does not have a spine?

_____

2. Giant squid sometimes eat other squid.

True   **False**

3. Why is there a school bus included in the infographic?

_____

4. One ton is equal to 2,000 pounds. About how many kilograms are equal to 2,000 pounds?

A. 900

B. 1,500

C. 2,000

D. 2,900

5. Why are giant squid rarely seen?

_____

Make a Pictograph

Draw a row of fish in the box to show how long an average giant squid is.

 = 3 feet

Make a Bar Graph

Use a standard ruler to measure 10 small objects. Round each measurement to the nearest $\frac{1}{2}$ inch. Shade in the bar graph below to record the length of each object. Then, answer the questions.

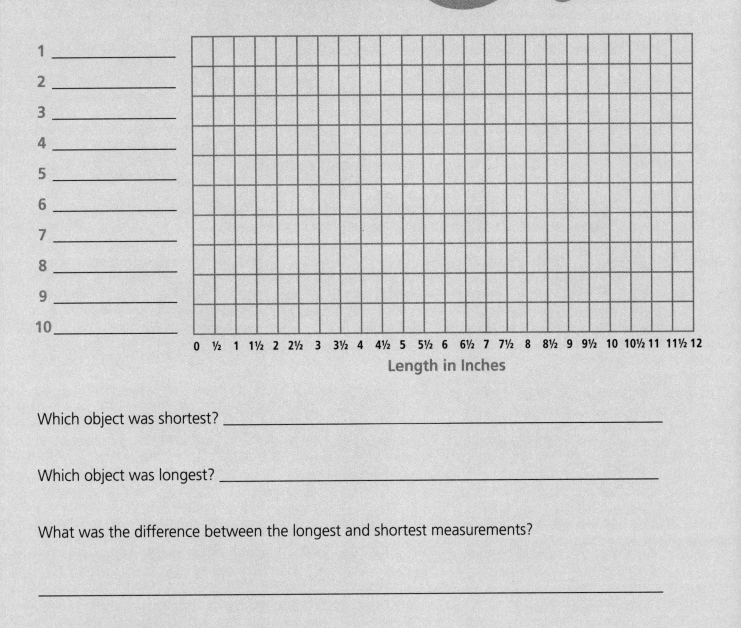

1 _____
2 _____
3 _____
4 _____
5 _____
6 _____
7 _____
8 _____
9 _____
10 _____

0   ½   1   1½   2   2½   3   3½   4   4½   5   5½   6   6½   7   7½   8   8½   9   9½   10   10½   11   11½   12

Length in Inches

Which object was shortest? _____

Which object was longest? _____

What was the difference between the longest and shortest measurements?

_____

Which two objects were the same length, or closest to the same length?

_____

Weird, Wonderful You!

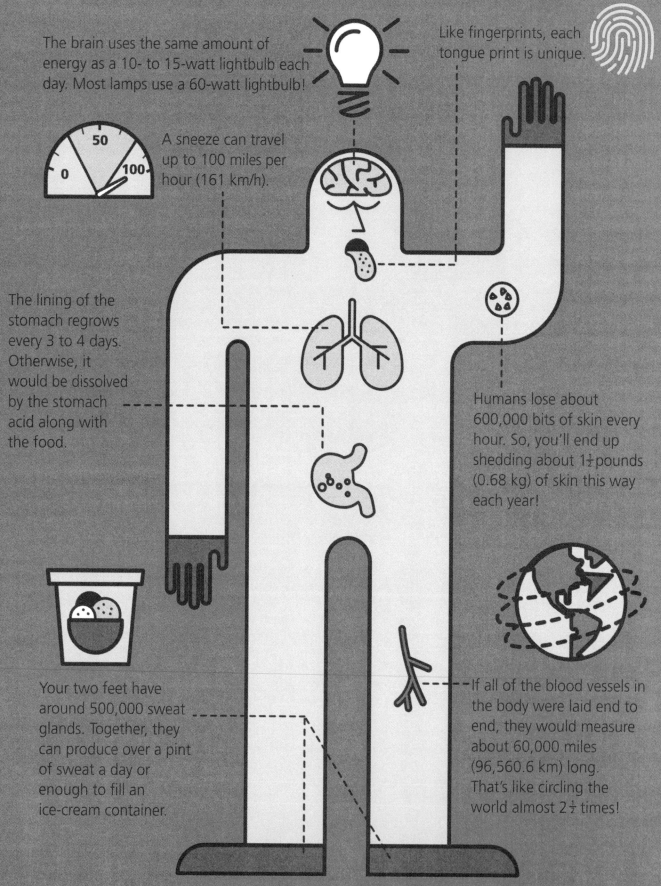

The brain uses the same amount of energy as a 10- to 15-watt lightbulb each day. Most lamps use a 60-watt lightbulb!

Like fingerprints, each tongue print is unique.

A sneeze can travel up to 100 miles per hour (161 km/h).

The lining of the stomach regrows every 3 to 4 days. Otherwise, it would be dissolved by the stomach acid along with the food.

Humans lose about 600,000 bits of skin every hour. So, you'll end up shedding about 1½ pounds (0.68 kg) of skin this way each year!

Your two feet have around 500,000 sweat glands. Together, they can produce over a pint of sweat a day or enough to fill an ice-cream container.

If all of the blood vessels in the body were laid end to end, they would measure about 60,000 miles (96,560.6 km) long. That's like circling the world almost 2½ times!

Piece It Together

Read the facts about the human body. Cut out the facts. Then, glue or tape them below the correct body system on page 61.

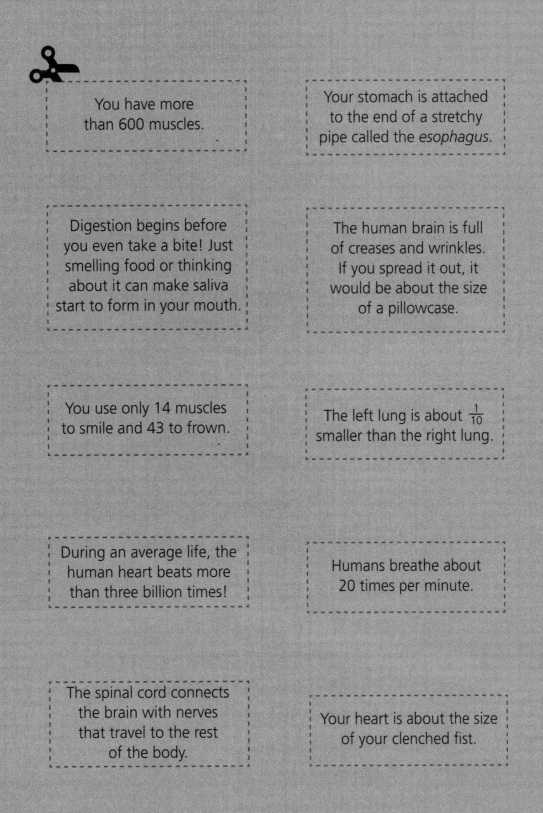

You have more than 600 muscles.

Your stomach is attached to the end of a stretchy pipe called the *esophagus*.

Digestion begins before you even take a bite! Just smelling food or thinking about it can make saliva start to form in your mouth.

The human brain is full of creases and wrinkles. If you spread it out, it would be about the size of a pillowcase.

You use only 14 muscles to smile and 43 to frown.

The left lung is about $\frac{1}{10}$ smaller than the right lung.

During an average life, the human heart beats more than three billion times!

Humans breathe about 20 times per minute.

The spinal cord connects the brain with nerves that travel to the rest of the body.

Your heart is about the size of your clenched fist.

Systems of the Human Body

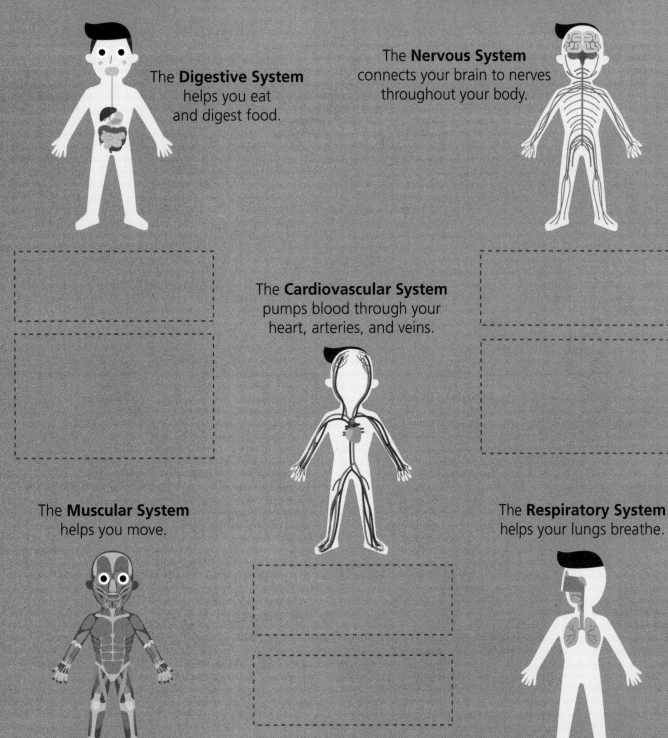

The **Digestive System** helps you eat and digest food.

The **Nervous System** connects your brain to nerves throughout your body.

The **Cardiovascular System** pumps blood through your heart, arteries, and veins.

The **Muscular System** helps you move.

The **Respiratory System** helps your lungs breathe.

Who Is Roy G. Biv?

Red

Orange

Yellow

Green

Blue

Indigo

Violet

The sun must be behind you in order to see a rainbow. This is because the light must reflect off the back of the drops and bounce back toward you.

White light

Sunlight

White light looks colorless, but it actually contains all the colors of the rainbow. When white light enters a prism, the light *refracts*, or bends. Each color of light bends at a slightly different angle. The colors of light are separated and the result is a rainbow.

A rainbow in the sky is caused by tiny raindrops. Each raindrop acts like a prism. White sunlight is refracted as it enters the raindrop. The colored light reflects off the back of the drop. The light is refracted again as it leaves the raindrop. If you are standing in the right place, you will see the refracted and reflected light from millions and millions of raindrops. That's the rainbow!

Think and Solve

Study the infographic. Answer the questions.

1. Which is an example of light refracting?

    A. light bouncing off a mirror

    B. light bending when it enters a prism

    C. sunlight blocked by a cloud

    D. light shining on water

2. True or false? In order to see a rainbow, the sun must be behind you.

_____

3. White light contains (all colors/no colors).

_____

4. In your own words, explain what causes a rainbow.

_____

_____

_____

_____

5. Who is Roy G. Biv?

_____

_____

_____

Color It

Color the rainbow. Make sure the colors are in the correct order.

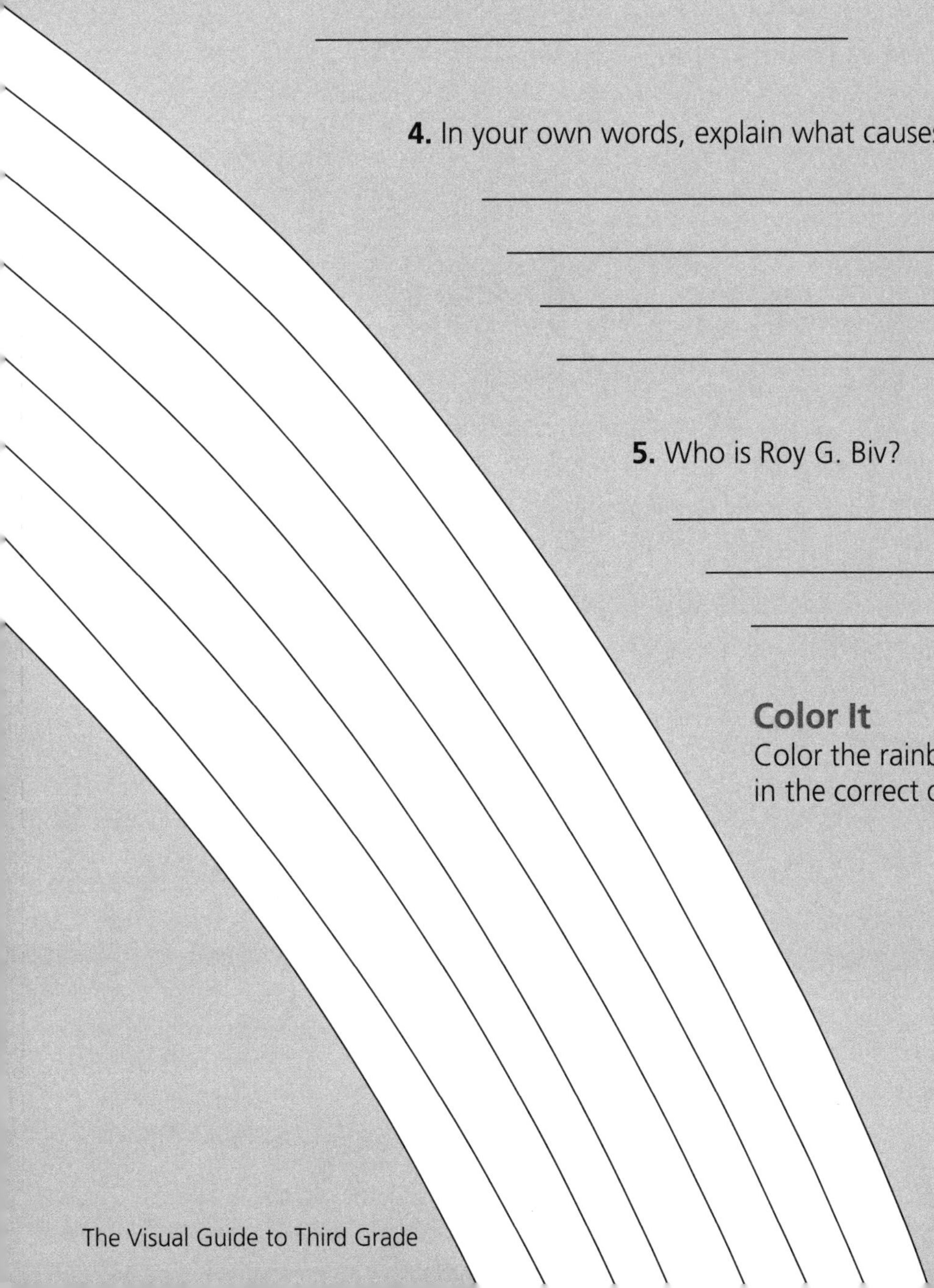

Water, Water Everywhere

When you see Earth from space, water appears to be the most abundant substance on our planet. So why is the availability of water such a big problem in so many parts of the world? It's because almost all of Earth's water is salt water. Humans need freshwater to survive.

 = about 97.5% of Earth's water is salt water

 = about 1.7% of Earth's water is frozen freshwater found in glaciers and at the ice caps

 = about 0.8% of Earth's water is unfrozen freshwater found in lakes, streams, or underground

World's 10 Largest Freshwater Lakes

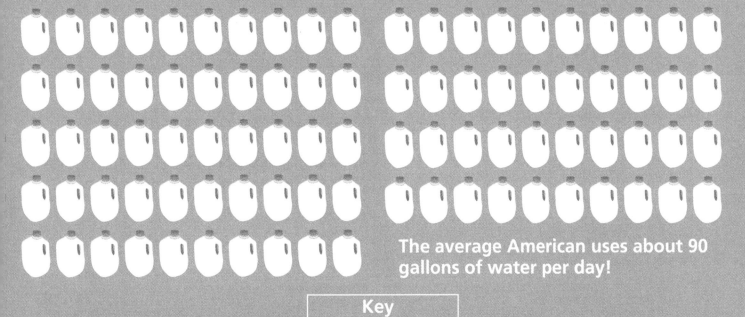

1. Lake Baikal
2. Lake Tanganyika
3. Lake Superior
4. Lake Nyasa
5. Lake Michigan
6. Lake Huron
7. Lake Victoria
8. Great Bear Lake
9. Great Slave Lake
10. Lake Ontario

How Much Water Do You Use Each Day?

The average American uses about 90 gallons of water per day!

Key

= 1 gallon

Log It
Use the chart below to keep track of about how much water you use in one day.
Read the facts to help you estimate how much water you use during different activities.

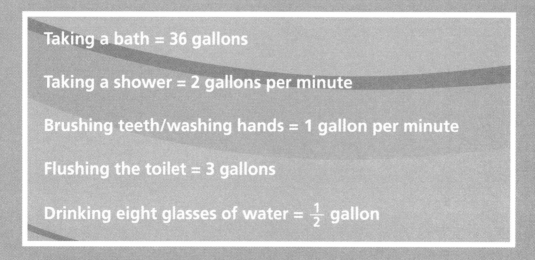

Taking a bath = 36 gallons

Taking a shower = 2 gallons per minute

Brushing teeth/washing hands = 1 gallon per minute

Flushing the toilet = 3 gallons

Drinking eight glasses of water = $\frac{1}{2}$ gallon

Activity I Did	Water I Used

Total =

Do you use more or less water than the average American?

Read About It: **Water Conservation**

ALTHOUGH OUR PLANET IS COVERED WITH WATER, most of it is salt water found in the ocean. There is a limited amount of usable freshwater in the world. We need freshwater to survive—so do the plants and animals that share Earth with us. Think about how people depend on water each day. We drink water, cook with it, wash with it, and use it to grow food. The population of the world is growing every day. The more people our planet supports, the more water we will need. It is important for each person to use water wisely and to *conserve* water (or keep from wasting it) as much as possible. How much water do you and your family use each day? How can you help conserve freshwater?

Try It Yourself

What can you do to use less water? It is easy for you and your family to make a difference. Read the suggestions below. Make a check mark next to the ones that you plan to do.

_____ Take a shower instead of a bath.

_____ Turn off the water while you brush your teeth.

_____ Ask your parents if your shower has a water-saving showerhead.

_____ Ask your parents if the toilets in your home are "low-flow."

_____ If you notice a leak or a drippy faucet, tell your parents
(or an adult at the place where you saw the leak).

_____ Collect rainwater and use it to water plants.

_____ Don't use the toilet as a trash can for tissues.
You waste water when you flush the toilet without needing to!

_____ If you wash dishes by hand, don't leave the water running between rinses.

_____ If you have a yard, encourage your parents to plant bushes
and plants that don't need a lot of water.

_____ Remind your parents to run the dishwasher and washing machine only for full loads.

_____ Tell friends and family members ways that they can use less water, too.

_____ If you play in the sprinkler, do it in a part of the yard that needs to be watered.

EVERY DROP COUNTS!

Inside the *Mayflower*

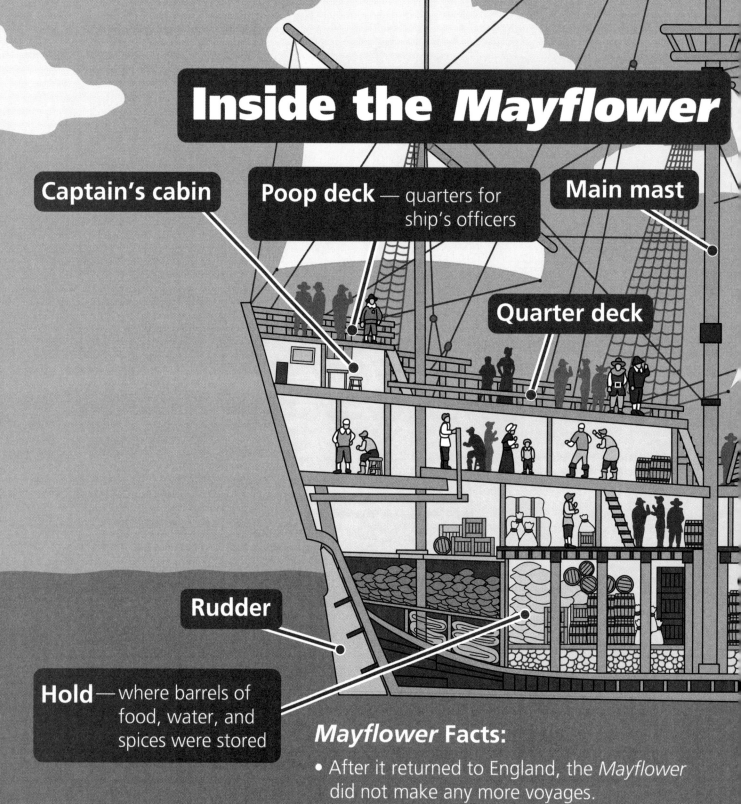

Captain's cabin

Poop deck — quarters for ship's officers

Main mast

Quarter deck

Rudder

Hold — where barrels of food, water, and spices were stored

Mayflower Facts:

- After it returned to England, the *Mayflower* did not make any more voyages.
- There were 102 passengers and 30 crew members aboard the *Mayflower*.
- One person died and one was born during the crossing. The baby was given the name Oceanus.

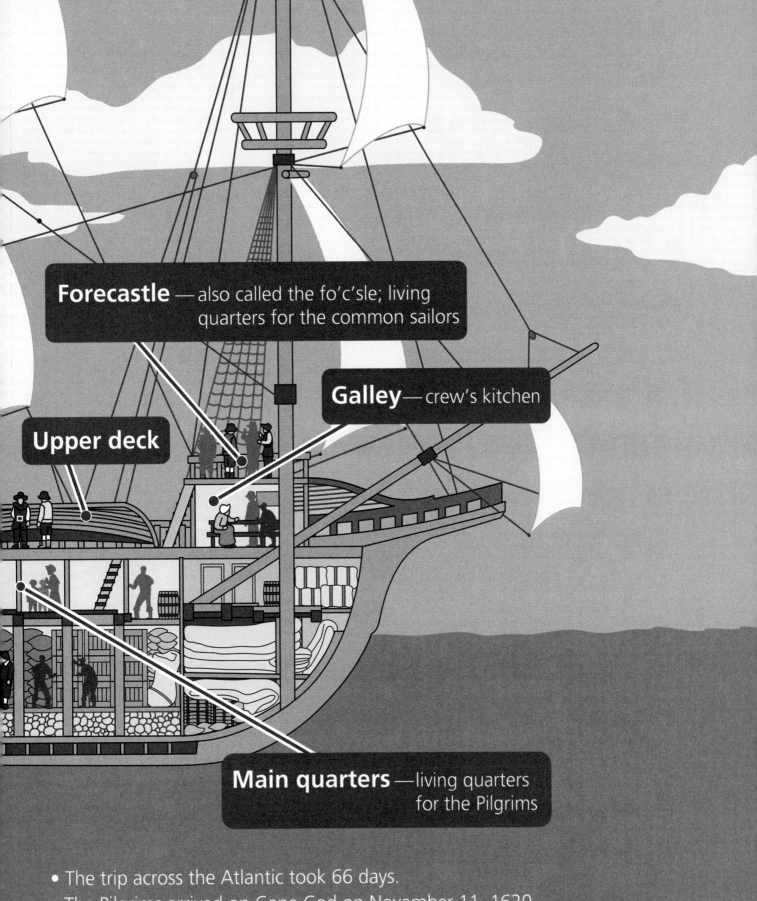

Forecastle—also called the fo'c'sle; living quarters for the common sailors

Galley—crew's kitchen

Upper deck

Main quarters—living quarters for the Pilgrims

- The trip across the Atlantic took 66 days.
- The Pilgrims arrived on Cape Cod on November 11, 1620. A few weeks later, they traveled on to Plymouth. They lived on the ship for a few more months while houses were built.

Think and Solve

Study the infographic. Answer the questions.

1. What was the galley?

   _____

2. Where did the ship's officers sleep?

   A. quarter deck

   B. poop deck

   C. upper deck

   D. forecastle

3. Where would food have been stored?

   A. in the main quarters

   B. in the hold

   C. on the quarter deck

   D. under the rudder

4. Why did the Pilgrims continue to live on the
   Mayflower for several months after it had reached land?

   _____

5. How many people sailed on the *Mayflower*?

   _____

6. Did the *Mayflower's* voyage take more or less than two months?

   _____

7. True or false? The forecastle is also called the *hold*.

   _____

8. Which was closer to the galley, the forecastle or the main mast?

   _____

9. True or false? The Pilgrims first landed at Plymouth and later traveled to Cape Cod.

   _____

10. Review the labeled diagram of a ship on page 29. How is that diagram similar
    to the diagram of the *Mayflower*? How are the two diagrams different?

    _____

    _____

    _____

Write About It

Imagine you are a passenger on the *Mayflower*. What is the journey like? What do you see on the ship or on the ocean? Why are you traveling to the new world?

On the lines below, write a diary entry describing a day on the *Mayflower*. Use at least three vocabulary words from the infographic. Be sure to include a date at the top of your entry.

Plants That Bite Back

Most plants get everything they need to grow from air, water, sunlight, and soil. But some plants live where the soil does not have enough minerals. In these places, some plants get the minerals they need by eating insects! They are called carnivorous plants. *Carnivorous* means "eats animals or insects."

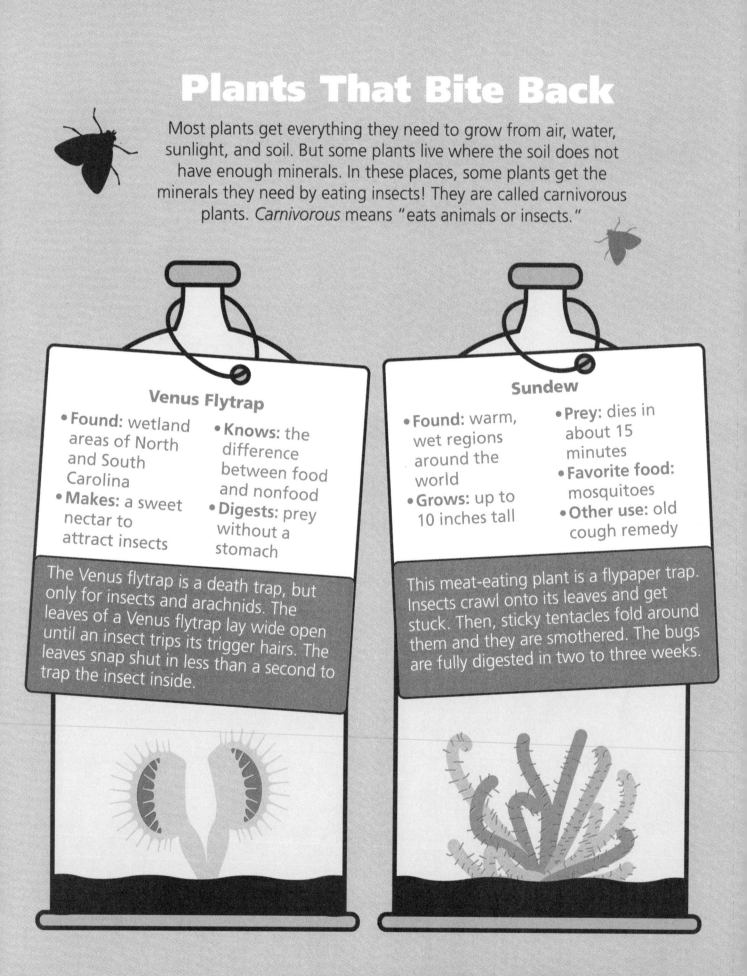

Venus Flytrap

- **Found:** wetland areas of North and South Carolina
- **Makes:** a sweet nectar to attract insects
- **Knows:** the difference between food and nonfood
- **Digests:** prey without a stomach

The Venus flytrap is a death trap, but only for insects and arachnids. The leaves of a Venus flytrap lay wide open until an insect trips its trigger hairs. The leaves snap shut in less than a second to trap the insect inside.

Sundew

- **Found:** warm, wet regions around the world
- **Grows:** up to 10 inches tall
- **Prey:** dies in about 15 minutes
- **Favorite food:** mosquitoes
- **Other use:** old cough remedy

This meat-eating plant is a flypaper trap. Insects crawl onto its leaves and get stuck. Then, sticky tentacles fold around them and they are smothered. The bugs are fully digested in two to three weeks.

Pitcher Plant

- **Found:** coastal states and Old World tropics
- **Size:** can be large enough to drown a rat
- **Favorite food:** mosquitoes
- **Other uses:** frogs may lay eggs inside; a bat motel

The pitcher plant looks like a pitcher half full of water. It draws insects in with its nectar, slippery parts, and bright color. Most insects drown. The more bugs they eat, the bigger pitcher plants get.

Bladderwort

- **Found:** lakes and streams around the world
- **Speed:** opens up and sucks in prey in $\frac{1}{35}$ of a second
- **Favorite foods:** insect larvae, tiny water worms, water fleas
- **Digests:** prey in 15 to 30 minutes

Bladderworts have no roots. They float in the water on several stems that grow out from the center. Tiny, balloon-like sacs, called *bladders*, grow along the stems. The little bladders are hollow, covered in hairs, and have a tiny opening. When prey gets close enough to touch a trigger hair, the bladder opens and sucks in water along with the insect.

Think and Solve

Study the infographic. Answer the questions.

1. Why do some plants need to eat insects?

_____

_____

2. Bladderworts are found only in wet areas of North and South Carolina.

True   **False**

3. A pitcher plant catches its prey by _____.

   A. drowning the insect with its nectar

   B. folding its sticky tentacles around it until it cannot breathe

   C. snapping its leaves shut, trapping the insect

   D. sucking the insect into a balloon-like sac

4. In the past, sundew plants were used as a cough remedy.

True   **False**

5. How does a Venus flytrap know when to trap an insect?

_____

6. Which phrase has the same meaning as *carnivorous*?

   A. eats nectar   **C.** looks like a balloon

   B. eats meat   **D.** looks like a pitcher

7. Write one fact about each plant.

Venus flytrap: _____

Sundew plant: _____

Pitcher plant: _____

Bladderwort: _____

8. How is a bladderwort different from the other three plants?

_____

9. Which plant would you like to find out more about and why?

_____

_____

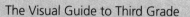

Draw and Write

Imagine you are a scientist who has just discovered a new kind of carnivorous plant. What does it look like? Where does it grow? What does it eat? Draw the plant in the jar below. Then, complete the label to describe your plant.

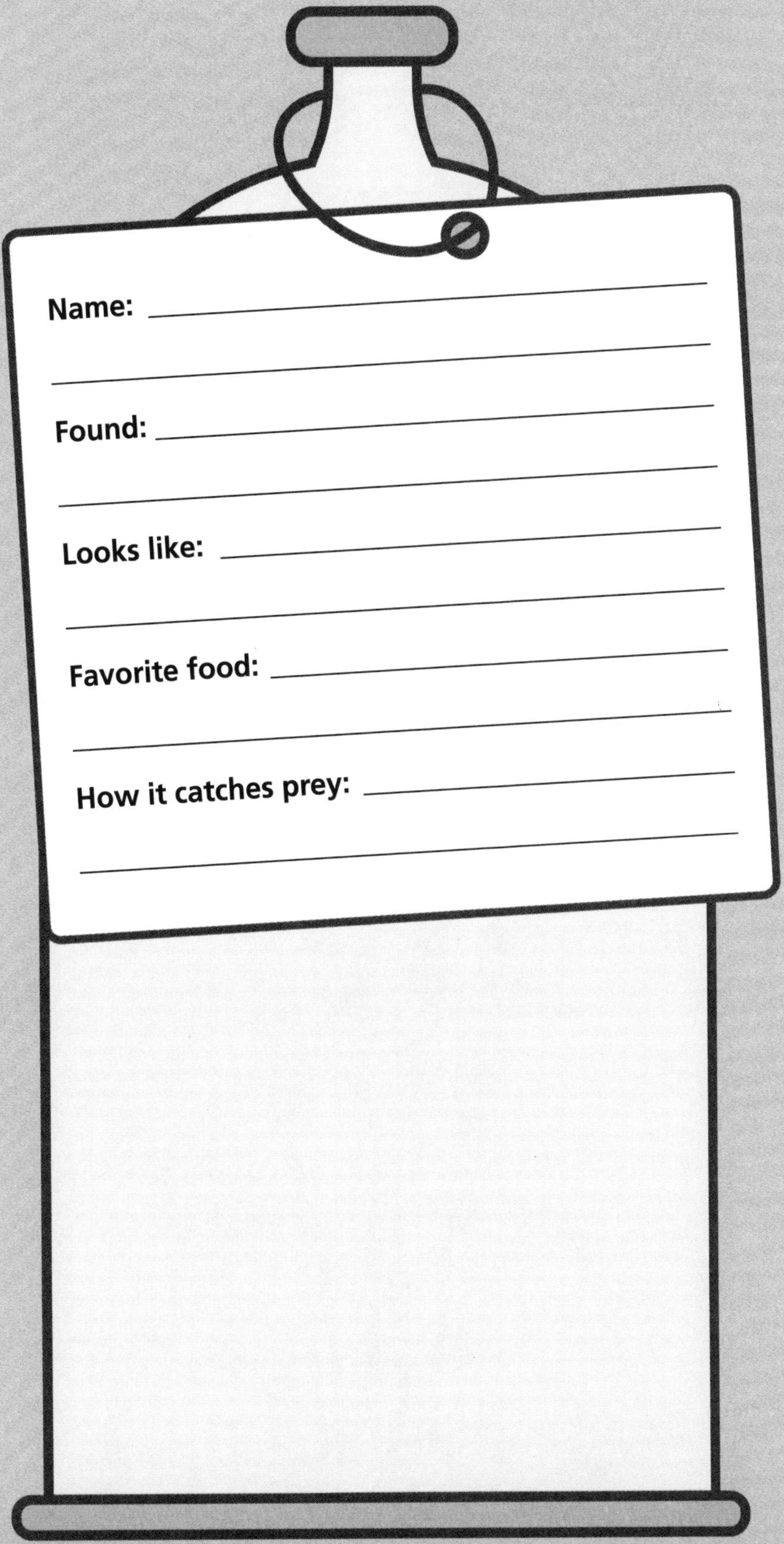

Name: _____

_____

Found: _____

_____

Looks like: _____

_____

Favorite food: _____

_____

How it catches prey: _____

_____

Dig Those Bones!

If you did not have bones, your body would be a squishy pile of muscles and organs. Your skeleton supports all the other parts of your body and helps you move around. Your bones also protect the important organs hard at work inside you.

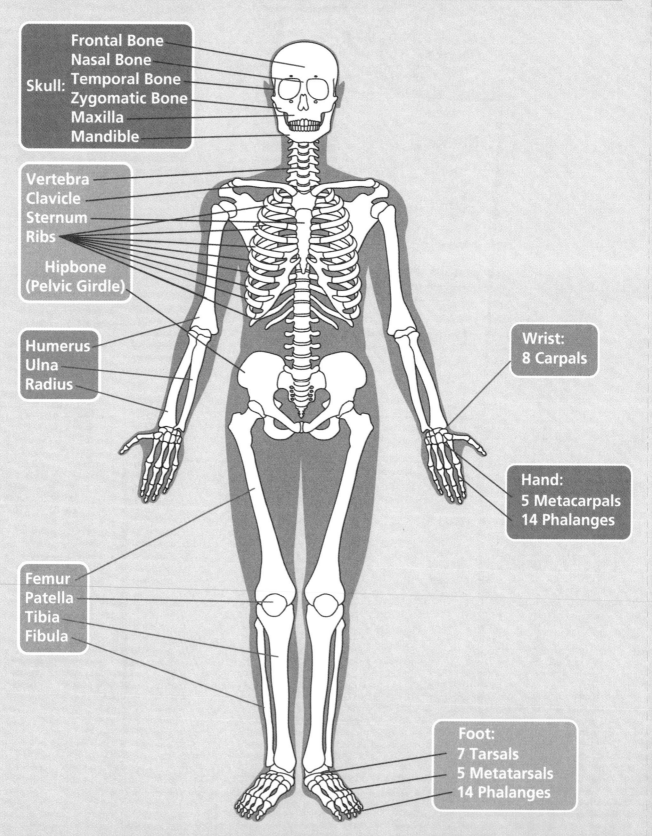

Skull:
Frontal Bone
Nasal Bone
Temporal Bone
Zygomatic Bone
Maxilla
Mandible

Vertebra
Clavicle
Sternum
Ribs

Hipbone
(Pelvic Girdle)

Humerus
Ulna
Radius

Wrist:
8 Carpals

Hand:
5 Metacarpals
14 Phalanges

Femur
Patella
Tibia
Fibula

Foot:
7 Tarsals
5 Metatarsals
14 Phalanges

An adult human skeleton has a total of 206 bones.

 The clavicle is the most commonly broken bone.

 Human babies are born with 300 bones, but as we mature, many of those bones fuse, or join, together.

 The hyoid is a U-shaped bone behind your tongue. It is the only bone that is not connected to other bones.

 Joints are the places where two bones meet and allow our bodies to bend and move.

 A broken bone takes about six to eight weeks to heal. Broken bones heal faster in children than in adults.

 There are 27 bones in each wrist and hand. Each foot contains 26 bones.

 Exercise and healthy eating lead to strong, healthy bones.

 The longest bone in the human body is the femur. An adult femur is about 50 cm long.

 The middle of a bone is called the *bone marrow*. It is where blood is made.

 The smallest bone in the human body is the stirrup. It is found deep inside the ear. It is only 3 millimeters long.

 Your spine, or backbone, is made up of 33 bones called *vertebrae*.

Think and Solve

Study the infographic. Answer the questions.

1. An adult human has more bones than a baby.

True   **False**

2. What is another name for your knee?

_____

3. How many phalanges are there in all four of your hands and feet?

   A. 14

   B. 28

   C. 42

   D. 56

4. What is a joint?

_____

5. The length of both femur bones is about _____ centimeters.

   A. 5

   B. 10

   C. 100

   D. 50

6. Which bone is not in the head?

   A. mandible

   B. clavicle

   C. maxilla

   D. hyoid

7. Blood is made inside your bones.

   True   **False**

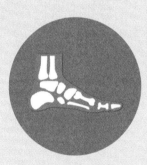

8. Which bone do people break most often?

_____

Piece It Together

The skeleton below was displayed in a classroom. The teacher accidentally knocked it over, and now it is in pieces. Can you put it back together the right way? Follow the lines to cut out each part of the skeleton. Then, glue or tape the pieces onto page 81 to create a complete skeleton.

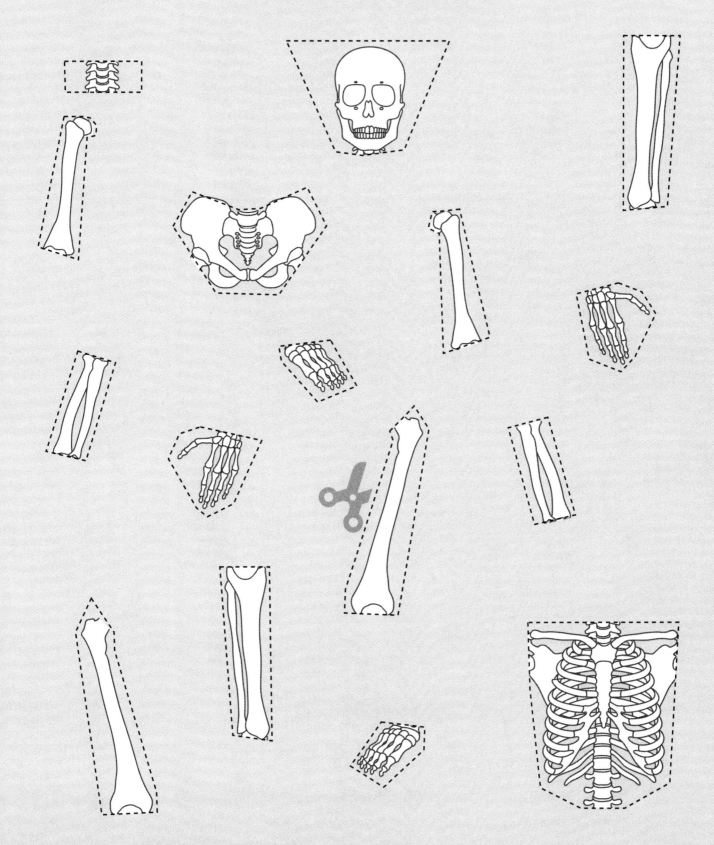

The Human Skeleton

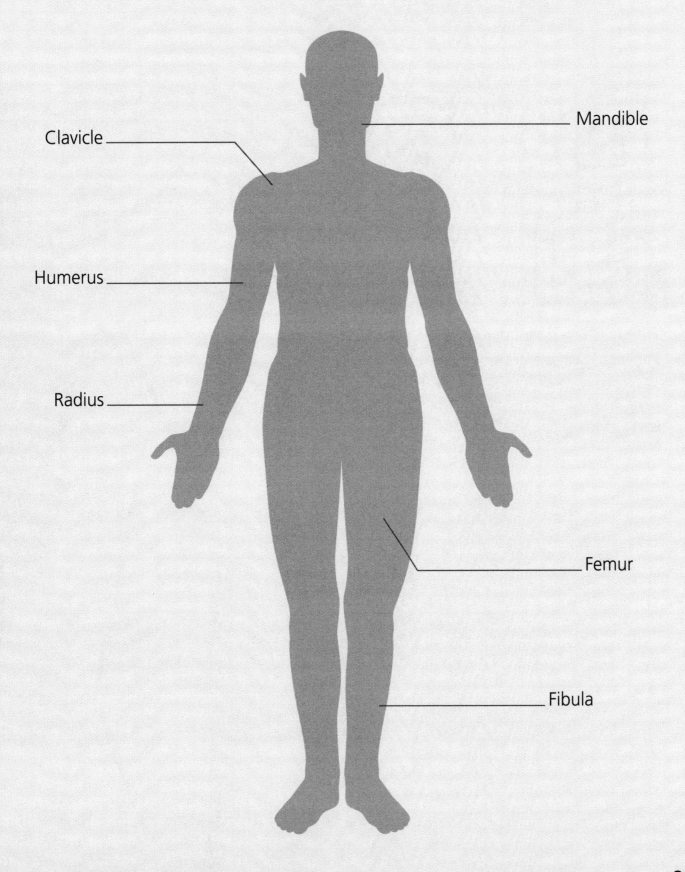

Mandible

Clavicle

Humerus

Radius

Femur

Fibula

Built to Survive

Cockroaches have a reputation for being the toughest living things around. They have survived for around 300 million years because they've been able to adapt and change no matter what. Read on to learn about some of their amazing adaptations.

Some roaches can survive for over a month without food and over a week without water. A cockroach can even survive for a week without its head. Scientists believe it dies only because it can't drink water.

A cockroach will eat anything to survive. It can even eat soap, glue, and leather.

Cockroaches breathe through holes in each of their three body segments— another reason they can survive so long without a head.

40 min.

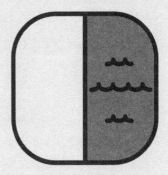

30 min.

A cockroach can hold its breath for up to 40 minutes. It can even stay under water for as long as 30 minutes.

200 mph

Roaches can run extremely fast for their size. Humans would have to run 200 miles per hour to be as fast at their size!

Some species can regrow limbs as they molt.

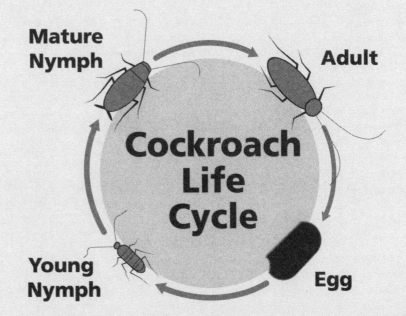

Mature Nymph

Adult

Cockroach Life Cycle

Young Nymph

Egg

Read About It:
Ladybugs

EVEN PEOPLE WHO DISLIKE INSECTS SEEM to have a soft spot for ladybugs. There is something about their cheery red bodies and black spots that makes them seem friendly.

They are sometimes known as *lady beetles* or *ladybird beetles*. No matter what they are called, these tiny spotted insects are helpful to humans. They eat insects, such as aphids, that are a threat to crops and gardens. As tiny as they are, they can eat up to 75 aphids a day.

Ladybugs are found all over the world, except in very cold places. Their spots and bright coloring tell other animals to stay away. They can secrete a terrible-tasting liquid if they are in danger. Most animals wouldn't make the mistake of trying to eat a ladybug more than once!

Ladybugs are often seen crawling from place to place, but they can fly. In fact, their wings beat about 85 times per second when they fly!

Ladybugs go through several stages of development. The female lays eggs on the backs of leaves. When the larvae hatch, they eat aphids for several weeks. They grow and shed their skin several times. Next, they enter a pupa stage in which they attach to a leaf and appear to sleep for several days. When they emerge from this stage, they are full-grown ladybugs.

Compare and Contrast

Complete the Venn diagram to compare and contrast cockroaches and ladybugs. Use facts from pages 82–84. Write facts about cockroaches in the circle on the left. Write facts about ladybugs in the circle on the right. In the overlapping section, write facts that are true about both insects.

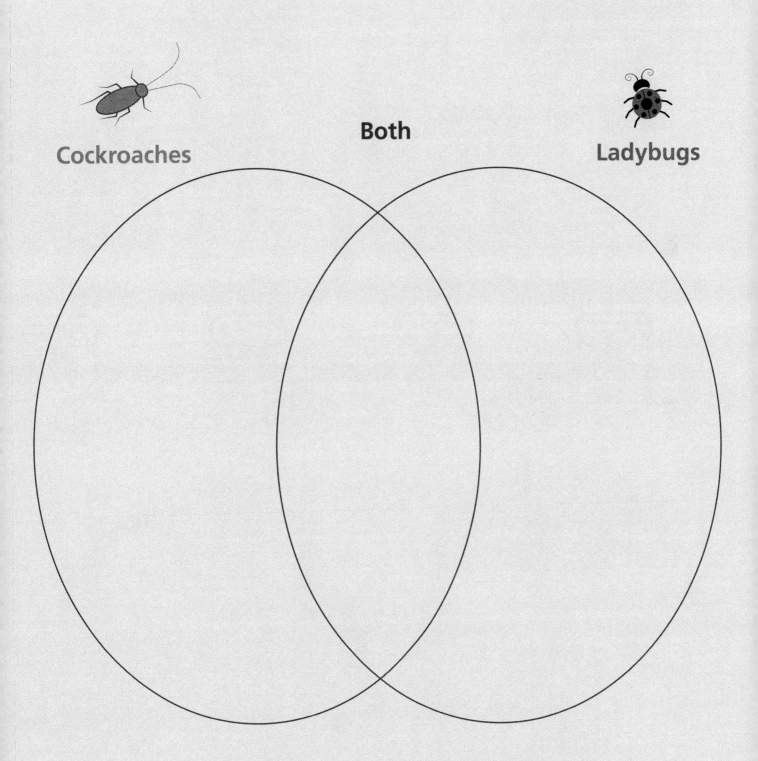

Cockroaches

Both

Ladybugs

Milestones in Early TV History

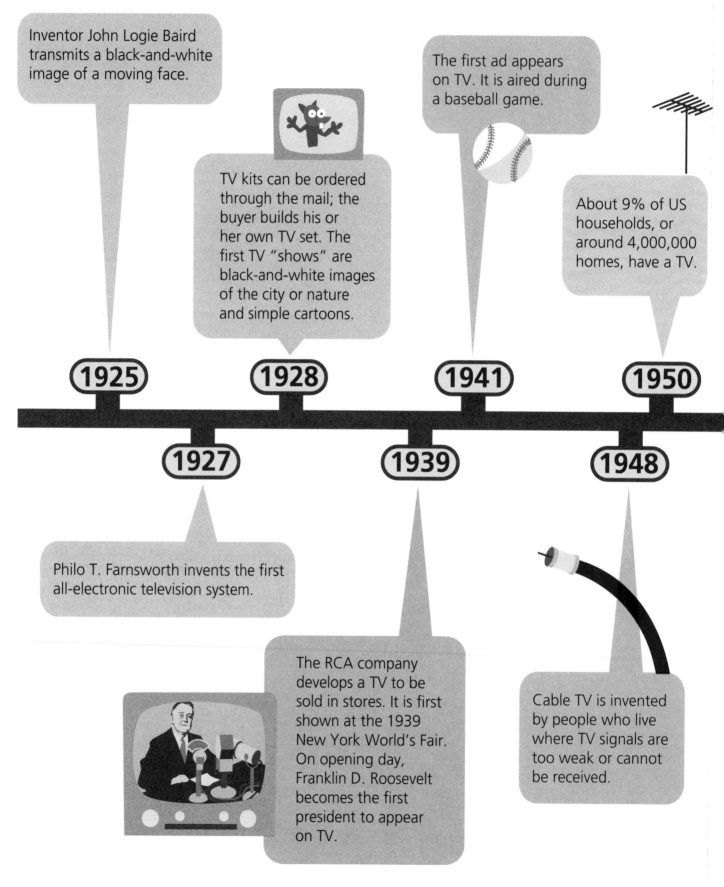

Inventor John Logie Baird transmits a black-and-white image of a moving face.

TV kits can be ordered through the mail; the buyer builds his or her own TV set. The first TV "shows" are black-and-white images of the city or nature and simple cartoons.

The first ad appears on TV. It is aired during a baseball game.

About 9% of US households, or around 4,000,000 homes, have a TV.

1925 **1928** **1941** **1950**

1927 **1939** **1948**

Philo T. Farnsworth invents the first all-electronic television system.

The RCA company develops a TV to be sold in stores. It is first shown at the 1939 New York World's Fair. On opening day, Franklin D. Roosevelt becomes the first president to appear on TV.

Cable TV is invented by people who live where TV signals are too weak or cannot be received.

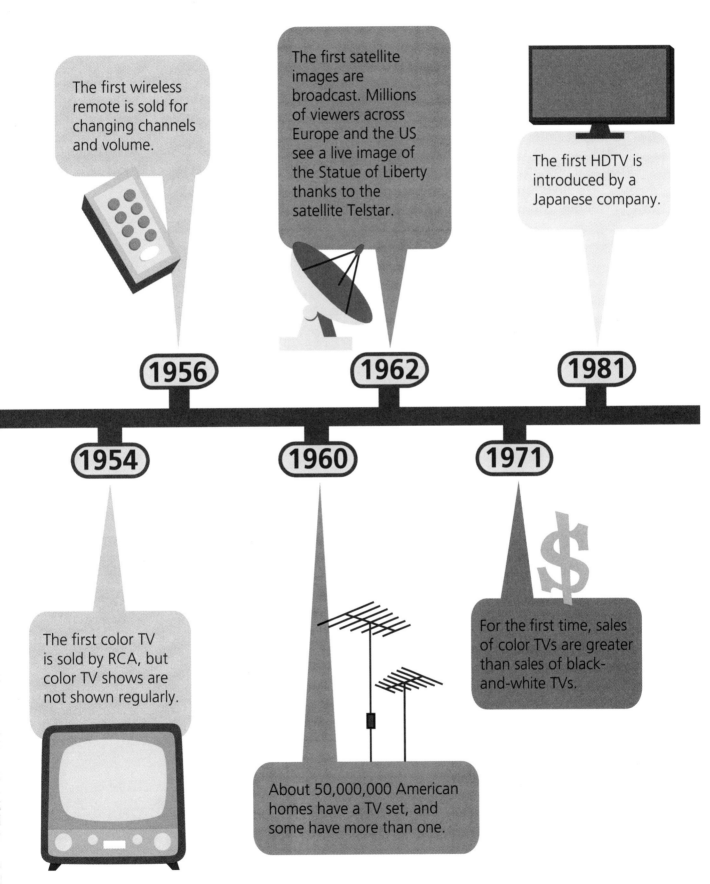

The first wireless remote is sold for changing channels and volume.

The first satellite images are broadcast. Millions of viewers across Europe and the US see a live image of the Statue of Liberty thanks to the satellite Telstar.

The first HDTV is introduced by a Japanese company.

1956

1962

1981

1954

1960

1971

The first color TV is sold by RCA, but color TV shows are not shown regularly.

About 50,000,000 American homes have a TV set, and some have more than one.

For the first time, sales of color TVs are greater than sales of black-and-white TVs.

Think and Solve

Study the infographic. Answer the questions.

1. True or false? The first color TV was shown at the 1939 World's Fair.

_____

2. Why was cable TV invented?

    A. to make the pictures look better

    B. to add sound to the pictures shown on TV

    C. to bring TV to people who could not get a signal

    D. to send pictures more quickly

3. The first satellite images were broadcast _____ years after cable TV was invented.

4. At least _____ American homes had a TV in 1950.

    A. five million   **C.** fifty million

    B. three and a half million   **D.** four and a half million

Log It

How much TV do you watch in one week? Use the chart below to keep track of the time you spend watching TV each day for a week. Round the amount of time to the nearest $\frac{1}{2}$ hour.

Day	Hours of TV Watching
Sunday	
Monday	
Tuesday	
Wednesday	
Thursday	
Friday	
Saturday	
Total for the Week:	

Do you think you spend too much time watching TV? Why or why not?

_____

_____

List activities you might choose to do instead of watching TV.

_____   _____   _____

_____   _____   _____

_____   _____   _____

Read About It:
How We Watch

TODAY, THERE ARE MANY CHOICES OF HOW TO WATCH TV. You might watch your favorite show on a computer, on a tablet, or on a 3-D television screen. But just 25 years ago, the choices were much more limited. Then, most families could watch only what was showing on a broadcast channel or cable channel. By the year 2000, nearly every home in the US had a VCR, or videocassette recorder and player. These devices allowed people to purchase or record shows and movies and choose when to watch them. DVDs and Blu-ray discs continued this trend. In 2002, more DVD players were sold than VCRs. By 2004, people had more choices than ever—there were more than 300 cable TV channels to choose from! Internet streaming services such as Netflix began in 2008, bringing even more TV-watching choices.

The devices we call TVs have also gone through many changes over time. In 1990, TVs were shaped like big, square boxes. The first widescreen, or rectangular, TVs went on sale in 1993. Two years later, the first flat-screen TVs became available. Today, most TV is shown in HDTV, or high-definition television. The picture is very clear and bright. The first show broadcast in HDTV was in 1998.

Make a Time Line
On the time line, write events described in the passage above. Draw a line from each event to the place on the time line that shows the year it happened.

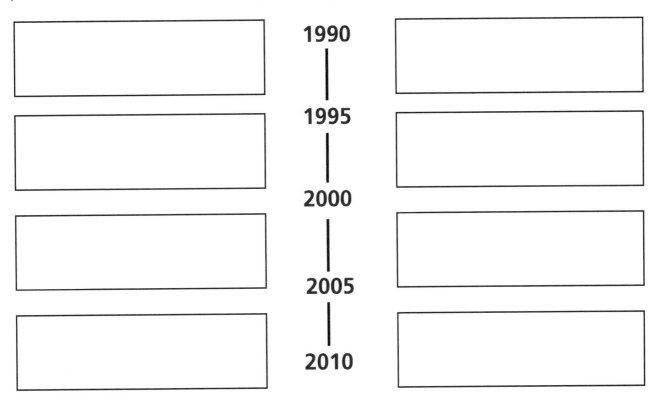

The Talented Mr. Franklin

His main trade in life was working as a printer and publisher, but this amazingly talented man also excelled at business, inventing, science, and politics.

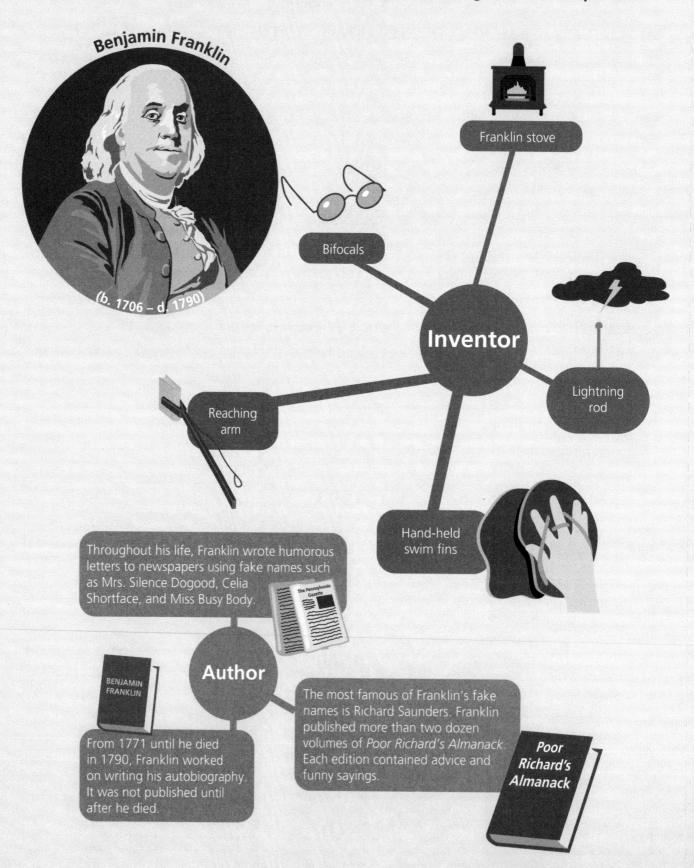

Benjamin Franklin

(b. 1706 – d. 1790)

Franklin stove

Bifocals

Inventor

Lightning rod

Reaching arm

Hand-held swim fins

Throughout his life, Franklin wrote humorous letters to newspapers using fake names such as Mrs. Silence Dogood, Celia Shortface, and Miss Busy Body.

The Pennsylvania Gazette

BENJAMIN FRANKLIN

Author

From 1771 until he died in 1790, Franklin worked on writing his autobiography. It was not published until after he died.

The most famous of Franklin's fake names is Richard Saunders. Franklin published more than two dozen volumes of *Poor Richard's Almanack*. Each edition contained advice and funny sayings.

Poor Richard's Almanack

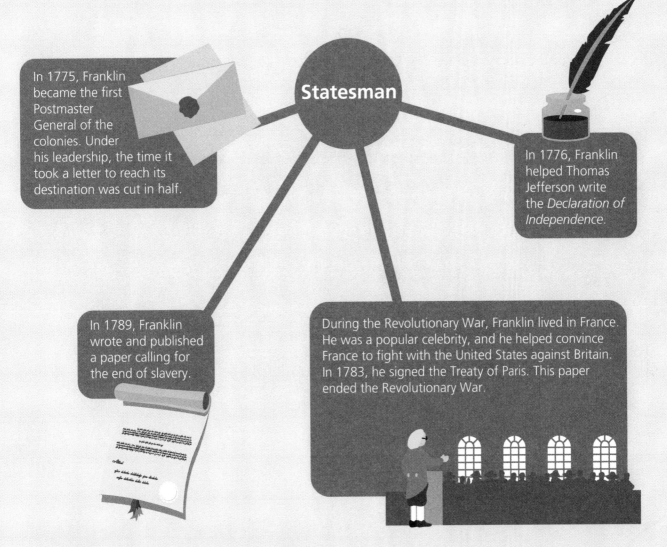

Statesman

In 1775, Franklin became the first Postmaster General of the colonies. Under his leadership, the time it took a letter to reach its destination was cut in half.

In 1776, Franklin helped Thomas Jefferson write the *Declaration of Independence*.

In 1789, Franklin wrote and published a paper calling for the end of slavery.

During the Revolutionary War, Franklin lived in France. He was a popular celebrity, and he helped convince France to fight with the United States against Britain. In 1783, he signed the Treaty of Paris. This paper ended the Revolutionary War.

Named for Ben

Benjamin Franklin is often called one of America's founding fathers. All kinds of things—from bridges to trees—have been named after him.

- **More than 80 towns, cities, and counties**
- **Dozens of schools (elementary through university)**
- **The Franklinia tree**
- **Benjamin Franklin Parkway (Philadelphia, PA)**
- **Mount Franklin (NH)**
- **Benjamin Franklin Bridge (Philadelphia, PA)**
- **Franklin Street (in at least five cities)**
- **The Franklin Crater on the moon**
- **The USS *Benjamin Franklin* submarine**

FRANKLIN STREET

Write About It

Many of Benjamin Franklin's sayings and words of wisdom are still read today. In fact, you may have heard some of them before. Read the quotes below from Franklin. Pick two. Use the lines to write about what each one means to you.

"Three may keep a secret, if two of them are dead."

"Early to bed and early to rise makes a man healthy, wealthy, and wise."

"When the well's dry, we know the worth of water."

"Little strokes fell great oaks."

"Does thou love life? Then do not squander time;
for that's the stuff life is made of."

"An ounce of prevention is worth a pound of cure."

"A penny saved is a penny earned."

Make Idea Webs
Read the adjective in the center of each web. On the lines, write facts and examples from Ben Franklin's life that show how the adjective describes him.

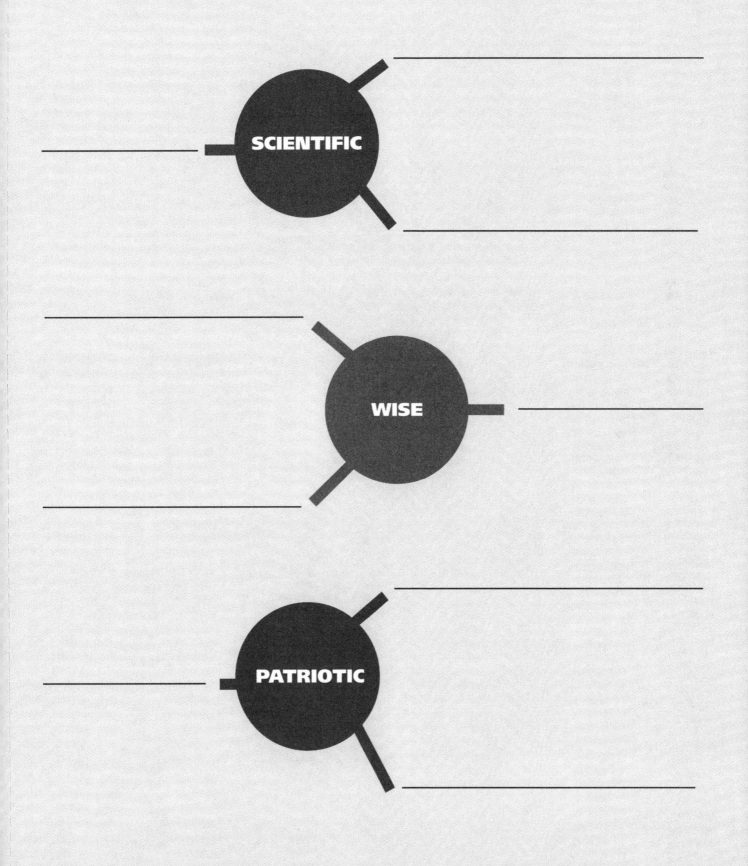

Far-Out Facts About the Moon

The Moon is Earth's only natural satellite. Humans have gazed at the Moon for thousands of years, telling stories and legends about it. The astronomer Galileo first saw the Moon with a telescope in 1610. More than 350 years later, humans walked on the Moon for the first time.

 Many scientists believe that the Moon formed billions of years ago when another planet crashed into Earth. Broken pieces of Earth flew into space and began orbiting. The broken pieces came together to form the Moon.

The Moon's gravity pulls on Earth. This pull makes the oceans bulge up toward the Moon as it passes over them. As Earth rotates, the oceans move up and down depending on where the Moon is. This movement is what causes tides.

 The Moon has no atmosphere, so there is no wind or weather on the Moon. The footsteps that the astronauts left behind in the Moon's dusty surface will be there for millions of years.

Gravity on the Moon is $\frac{1}{6}$ as strong as gravity on Earth. That means if you weigh 72 pounds on Earth, you will weigh only 12 pounds on the Moon!

 The Moon is about 240,000 miles from Earth.

 The Moon travels around Earth at about 2,300 miles per hour!

 The Moon doesn't have any air around it. For this reason, it gets much hotter and colder than Earth. On the side where the Sun is shining, it reaches about 260°F. On the dark side of the Moon, temperatures dip to about 280°F below zero!

Phases of the Moon

As the Moon travels around Earth, its position changes in relation to the Sun and Earth. At different times, we see the bright parts of the Moon's surface at different angles. These are called *phases of the Moon*. It takes about one month to see all the Moon's phases.

					1	2
3 Full Moon	**4**	**5**	**6**	**7**	**8**	**9**
10	**11**	**12** Last Quarter Moon	**13**	**14**	**15**	**16**
17	**18** New Moon	**19**	**20**	**21**	**22**	**23**
24	**25** Full Quarter Moon	**26**	**27**	**28**	**29**	**30**

In American folklore, the full Moon for each month has been given a nickname.

January
Wolf Moon

February
Snow Moon

March
Worm Moon

April
Pink Moon

May
Flower Moon

June
Strawberry Moon

July
Buck Moon

August
Sturgeon Moon

September
Corn Moon

October
Hunter's Moon

November
Beaver Moon

December
Cold Moon

The Moon's orbit around Earth takes about 28 days. At the same time, the Moon is also rotating, or spinning. The Moon makes one full spin about every 28 days, too. Since one orbit and one full spin take the same amount of time, that means the same side of the Moon is always facing Earth! The "dark side" of the Moon is the side we never see.

Think and Solve

Study the infographic. Answer the questions.

1. True or false? The Moon is both hotter and colder than Earth.

_____

2. Which of the following is not a nickname for a full Moon?

  A. crescent moon

  B. wolf moon

  C. strawberry moon

  D. worm moon

3. Why do we never see the "dark side" of the Moon from Earth?

_____

_____

4. Why is there no wind or weather on the Moon?

_____

_____

Read About It: **Waxing and Waning**

EACH DAY OF THE MONTH, a different amount of the Moon is lit by the Sun. To our eyes on Earth, it looks like the Moon is changing shape. The changes in the way the Moon appears are called the *phases of the Moon*. It takes the Moon about $29 \frac{1}{2}$ days to go through its eight phases. The phases are New, New Crescent, First Quarter, Waxing Gibbous, Full, Waning Gibbous, Last Quarter, and Old Crescent. (*Waxing* means "increasing in size," and *waning* means "decreasing in size.") If you visit www.almanac4kids.com/sky/thismonth.php, you can see what phase the Moon is in on any night of the year.

Explore Your World

Fill in the dates on the calendar below for the next 30 days. Observe the Moon each night for a month. Draw a sketch of the Moon in the box for each day on the calendar. Label the days that show the best examples of the eight phases of the Moon.

SUNDAY	MONDAY	TUESDAY	WEDNESDAY	THURSDAY	FRIDAY	SATURDAY

Make a Pictograph

Make a pictograph to show the number of miles between Earth and the Moon. In the box, draw one star for each 10,000 miles.

 = 10,000 miles

Seven Natural Wonders of the World

North America

South America

Grand Canyon

From 175 yards (160 m) at its narrowest to 18 miles (29 km) at its widest, the Grand Canyon winds through Arizona for about 277 miles (446 km). At its deepest, it is more than 6,000 feet (1,800 m) from the rim to the bottom of the canyon.

Parícutin Volcano

This is one of the youngest volcanoes on Earth. It was "born" and began erupting on February 20, 1943. The last eruptions occurred in 1952, after reaching a height of 9,210 feet (2,808 m).

Harbor at Rio de Janeiro

Surrounded by mountains and islands, the bay is the largest in the world by volume. It is about 19 miles (31 km) by 18 miles (29 km) at its widest points.

The Northern Lights

Also called *aurora borealis*, these naturally occurring lights often appear as waves, arcs, or bands of greenish light that dance across the sky. They generally occur from 50 to 155 miles (80 to 250 km) above the surface of Earth.

Asia

Europe

Mount Everest

The highest spot on the surface of Earth, it reaches 29,029 feet (8,850 m) at its summit. The mountain is also known as *Chomolungma* in Tibetan, meaning "Goddess Mother of the World," or "Goddess of the Valley."

Africa

Australia

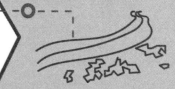

Victoria Falls

It is no wonder that locals call the largest waterfall in the world *Mosi-oa-Tunya*, which means "smoke that thunders." The falls are 1 mile (1.7 km) wide and 360 feet (108 m) high. On average, almost 33,000 cubic feet (935 m³) of water fall each second.

Great Barrier Reef

The Great Barrier Reef is the largest formation in the world created by living organisms. At over 1,600 miles (2,600 km) long, it can be seen from space. It includes over 2,900 separate reefs and 900 islands.

Antarctica

Think and Solve
Study the infographic. Answer the questions.

1. True or false? The Parícutin Volcano in Mexico gets its name from a Native American word meaning "smoke that thunders."

_____

2. The Great Barrier Reef was created by _____.

    A. a volcano

    B. an earthquake

    C. a tsunami

    D. living organisms

3. Which continent is not home to one of the seven natural wonders of the world?

_____

4. One mile is equal to 5,280 feet. About how many miles tall is Mount Everest?

    A. $4\frac{1}{2}$ miles

    B. 5 miles

    C. $5\frac{1}{2}$ miles

    D. 6 miles

5. How many cubic feet of water fall at Victoria Falls every 10 seconds?

    A. 33,000 cubic feet

    B. 330,000 cubic feet

    C. 3,300,000 cubic feet

    D. 33,000,000 cubic feet

6. The last eruptions of the Parícutin Volcano occurred _____ years ago.

7. You are in Canada viewing the Northern Lights. Describe what you see.

_____

_____

8. Which expression could be used to find the area of the Harbor at Rio de Janeiro?

    A. 19 × 18

    B. 19 ÷ 18

    C. 18 + 1

    D. 19 − 18

Piece It Together

Study the shapes of the continents below. Write the name of each continent on the line. Then, cut out the continents. Glue or tape them in place on page 103 to make a world map.

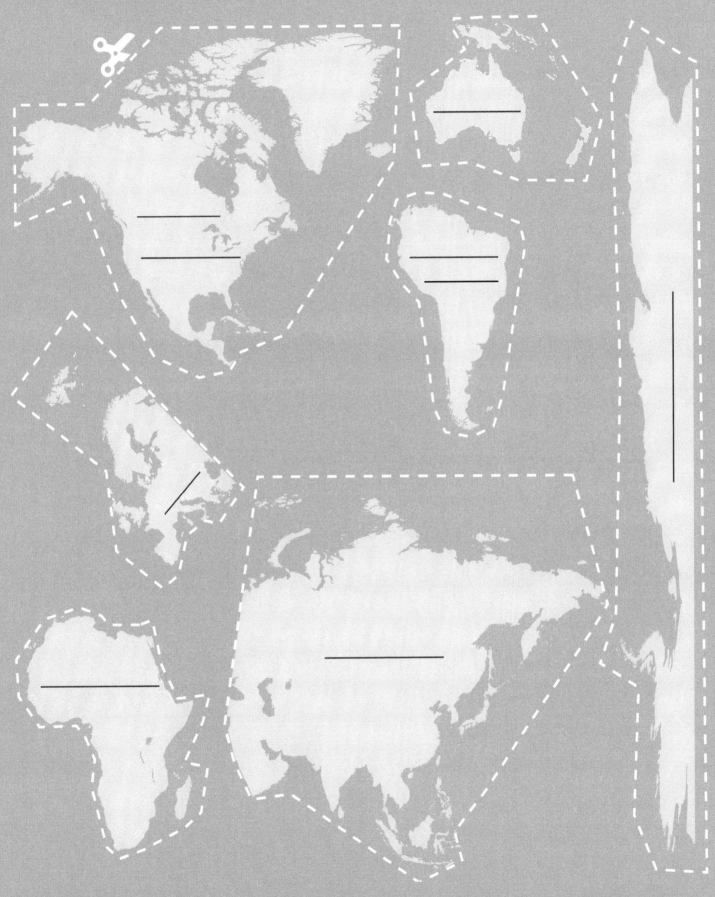

The Visual Guide to Third Grade

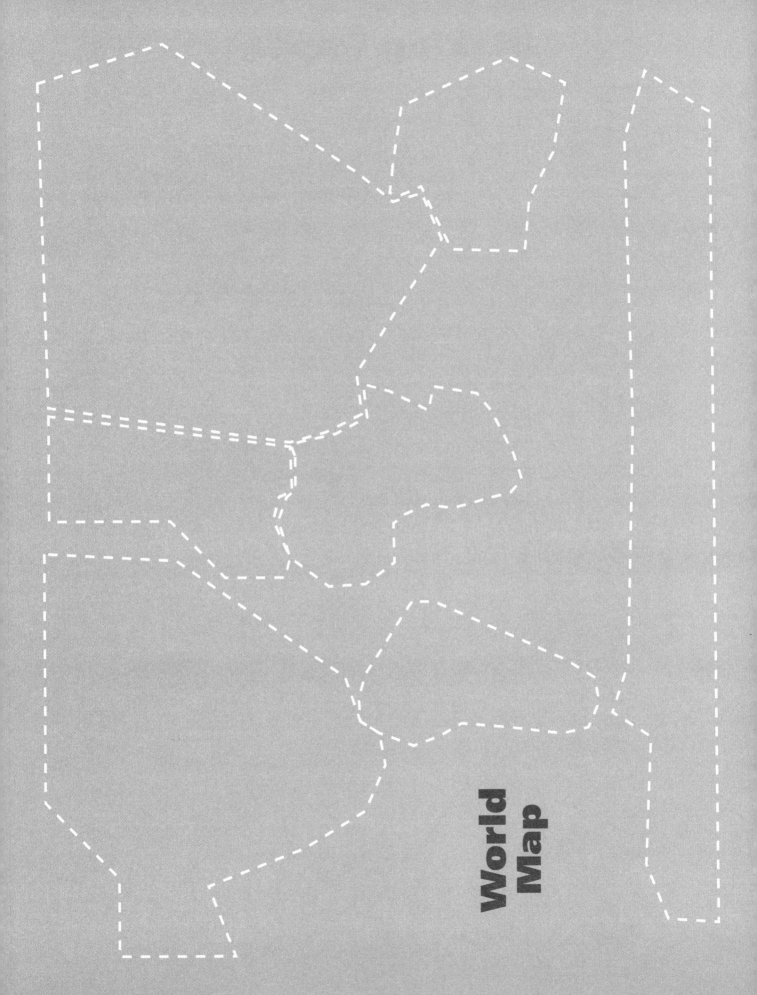

World
Map

Making Paper

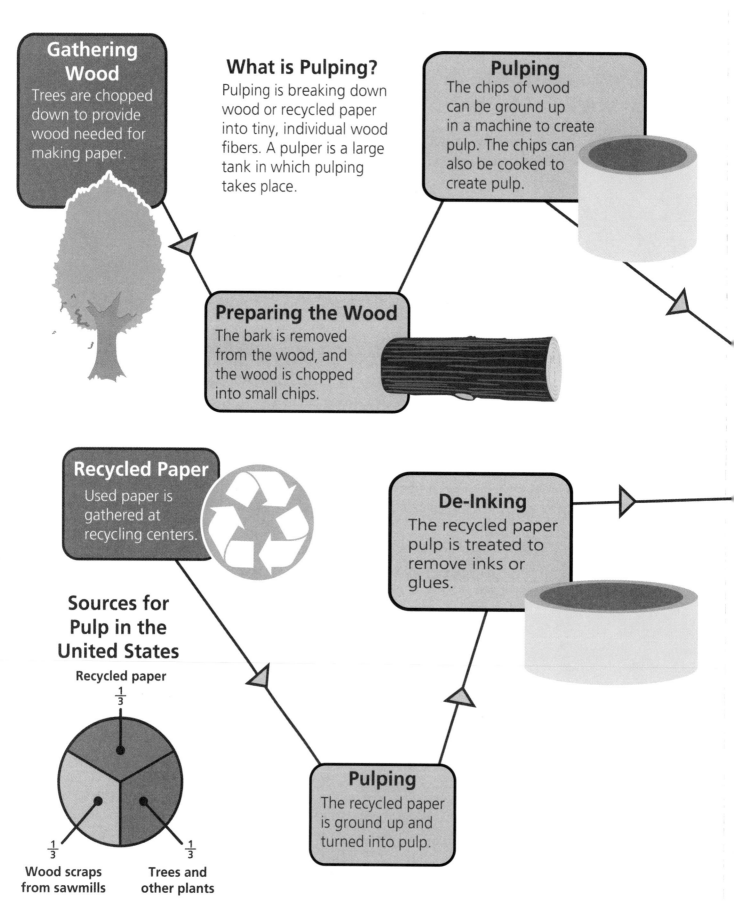

Gathering Wood
Trees are chopped down to provide wood needed for making paper.

What is Pulping?
Pulping is breaking down wood or recycled paper into tiny, individual wood fibers. A pulper is a large tank in which pulping takes place.

Pulping
The chips of wood can be ground up in a machine to create pulp. The chips can also be cooked to create pulp.

Preparing the Wood
The bark is removed from the wood, and the wood is chopped into small chips.

Recycled Paper
Used paper is gathered at recycling centers.

De-Inking
The recycled paper pulp is treated to remove inks or glues.

Sources for Pulp in the United States

Recycled paper
$\frac{1}{3}$

$\frac{1}{3}$
Wood scraps from sawmills

$\frac{1}{3}$
Trees and other plants

Pulping
The recycled paper is ground up and turned into pulp.

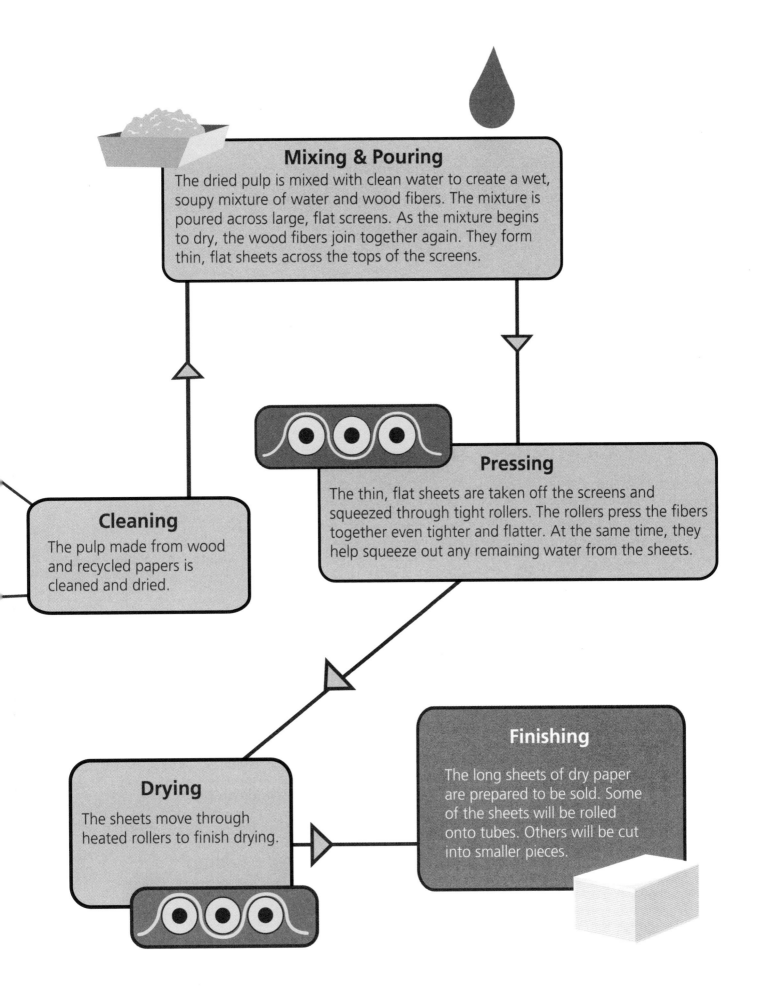

Mixing & Pouring

The dried pulp is mixed with clean water to create a wet, soupy mixture of water and wood fibers. The mixture is poured across large, flat screens. As the mixture begins to dry, the wood fibers join together again. They form thin, flat sheets across the tops of the screens.

Pressing

The thin, flat sheets are taken off the screens and squeezed through tight rollers. The rollers press the fibers together even tighter and flatter. At the same time, they help squeeze out any remaining water from the sheets.

Cleaning

The pulp made from wood and recycled papers is cleaned and dried.

Finishing

The long sheets of dry paper are prepared to be sold. Some of the sheets will be rolled onto tubes. Others will be cut into smaller pieces.

Drying

The sheets move through heated rollers to finish drying.

Think and Solve
Study the infographic. Answer the questions.

1. List three sources of pulp for papermaking.

_____

_____

_____

2. The purpose of de-inking is to remove _____ and _____.

3. True or false? Recycled paper does not need to be pulped.

_____

4. Which step is needed to prepare recycled paper pulp that is not needed when preparing wood pulp?

_____

5. Which happens first: pressing or drying?

_____

Try It Yourself
Read the list of things to make or do. Make a check mark beside one thing that you can explain how to make or do.

☐ making a sandwich

☐ making a paper airplane

☐ making a friendship bracelet

☐ making a birdfeeder

☐ making pancakes

☐ making a sun catcher

☐ making a model volcano

☐ making a snowman

☐ getting a baby to sleep

☐ checking out a library book

☐ riding a scooter

☐ taking a photograph

Make a Process Chart

Think about the choice you made on page 106. Use the chart below to explain each step you need to follow to make or do that thing. Draw and write one step in each space. Write a title at the top.

How to: _____

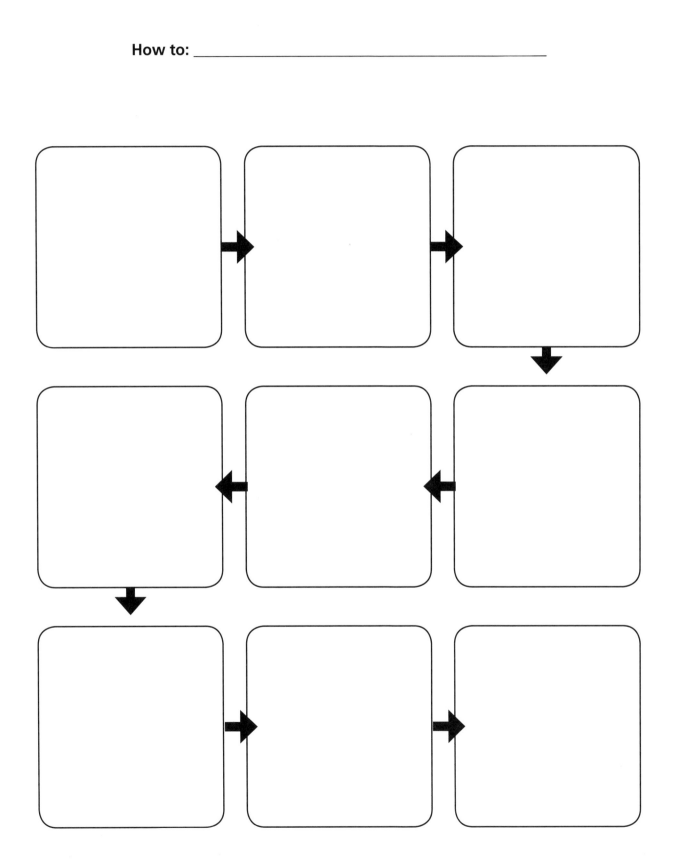

Miles Above Earth

The International Space Station is a human-made satellite that orbits Earth. It was built so that astronauts could have a place to do research and experiments in space. It is the largest artificial body orbiting Earth.

The space station is being built piece by piece. The first part, the Zarya module, was put into orbit in 1998 by the Russians.

The ISS* travels at a speed of more than 17,000 miles (or about 28,000 km) per hour.

 When the ISS is complete, more than 90% of people around the world will be able to see it.

 It has cost more to build the space station than any other single project ever.

 Aside from the Moon, the space station is the brightest object in the night sky.

 The ISS floats about 240 miles above Earth.

 Humans don't need as much sleep in space as on Earth. Without gravity, work takes much less effort!

The ISS weighs about 925,000 pounds!

The ISS has a gym so that astronauts can work out daily and stay fit.

Electricity on the ISS travels through more than eight miles of wires.

Fifty-two computers control the ISS.

*ISS stands for the International Space Station.

More than 200 people have visited the space station since 2000.

Sixteen countries, including the US and Russia, are working together to build the space station.

The living/working space in the ISS is about equal to the size of two airplanes.

It takes about an hour and a half for the space station to circle Earth. It can complete about 16 orbits per day.

An ATV is an unmanned spacecraft. It can bring supplies like food and fuel to the astronauts living on the ISS.

Study the infographic. Answer the questions.

1. How many minutes does it take for the ISS to circle Earth?

_____

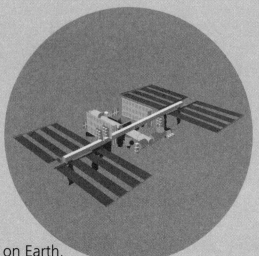

2. The Zarya module was the _____.

    A. first piece of the ISS to go into orbit

    B. main computer in the ISS

    C. only piece of the space station built by Russians

    D. last piece of the ISS to go into orbit

3. True or false? Humans need more sleep in space than they do on Earth.

_____

4. Review the speed at which the ISS travels. Based on this information, which is longer, a mile or a kilometer?

_____

5. Visit http://spotthestation.nasa.gov/sightings/. This NASA website tells you where and when you can spot the ISS. Enter your location, and record the time and date you will next be able to see it in orbit.

_____

Read About It: **Science in Space**

ONE OF THE MAIN MISSIONS OF THE ISS ASTRONAUTS is to perform experiments. Many of the experiments are designed to find out how life in space is different than life on Earth. In one experiment, a variety of microbes (microscopic germs) were sent to the ISS to see how they would grow. The same microbes were grown on Earth so scientists could make a comparison.

    In another experiment, a colony of ants was sent into space so scientists could observe their behavior. The way the ants behave in new conditions may help scientists design robots for space exploration.

Design an Experiment

Imagine that your school is having a contest. Each student must design a science experiment that can be performed on the ISS. The winning experiment will be performed in space! Fill in the graphic organizer below with the details of your experiment.

Hypothesis (the idea you want to test) _____

_____

_____

Equipment (the materials you will need) _____

_____

_____

_____

Method (what steps should be taken to perform the experiment)

_____

_____

_____

_____

_____

_____

_____

_____

_____

_____

Prediction (what you think will happen) _____

_____

_____

_____

_____

Left Behind

What is a fossil?
A fossil is the ancient remains of a plant or animal. Usually, only the hard parts (like shells, bones, and teeth) are preserved.

How do fossils form?

A fish swims in the prehistoric sea.

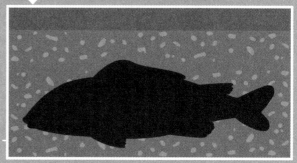

The fish dies and sinks to the sea floor. Some parts are eaten by other animals. The other soft parts decompose.

Only the skeleton remains. Over time, it is buried by mud and sand.

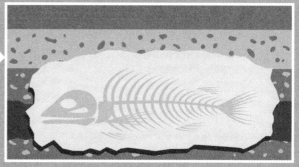

The layers of mud and silt eventually turn into sedimentary rock. The skeleton dissolves, which leaves a space or mold in the rock. The mold fills with minerals. They create a fossil in the shape of the skeleton.

Common Fossils			
Name	ammonites	trilobites	brachiopods	shark teeth
Animal	sea creatures related to squids and octopuses	sea creatures related to crabs; bodies had three (tri) parts	sea creatures with two shells, similar to oysters	sharks, similar to modern day sharks; lost many teeth in a lifetime, so fossils are common
Age	65–200 million years	250–540 million years	65–540 million years	37–56 million years

Sequence It

Number the steps 1–6 to show the order in which a fossil is formed.

_____ Mud and silt turn into stone.

_____ The animal's skeleton dissolves.

_____ An animal dies.

_____ The animal's skeleton is covered in mud and silt.

_____ Minerals fill in the spaces where the skeleton used to be.

_____ Soft parts of the animal's body dissolve.

Make a Time Line

On the time line, draw a colored line for each common fossil to show the span of years when the animal would have been alive.

AMMONITES	————
TRILOBITES	————
BRACHIOPODS	————
SHARK TEETH	————

Millions of Years Ago

550	500	450	400	350	300	250	200	150	100	50

Explore Your World

On a walk or hike, collect rocks. Choose the most interesting rocks you find and record details about them in the chart below.

	Size in cm	Color	Interesting details
Rock #1			
Rock #2			
Rock #3			
Rock #4			
Rock #5			

Sea Turtles

50 years

ago, the Kemp's ridley was almost extinct.

Turtles can lay more than

150 eggs

per clutch.

Green sea turtles can stay under water for a long time during a feeding dive. Heartbeats may be up to

9 minutes apart.

Most sea turtles migrate long distances between their feeding grounds and nesting grounds. Some travel

1,400 miles!

Sea turtles have been around approximately

110 million years!

Leatherback turtles can weigh more than

2,000 pounds.

Only about one in

1,000

sea turtle eggs will make it to adulthood.

Green sea turtles are protected in Florida. In 2013, there were more than

25,000

green sea turtle nests on Florida beaches.

6 out of 7

types of sea turtles have hard shells. Only leatherback turtles do not.

Sea turtles can live to be

80 - 100 years old.

Some sea turtles can hold their breath for

30 minutes

during a dive.

Hawksbill turtles live and feed in coral reefs. One turtle can eat

1,000 pounds

of sea sponges per year.

VU
Vulnerable

A species with a high risk of extinction

- Leatherback
- Olive ridley
- Flatback

EN
Endangered

A species with a very high risk of extinction

- Green turtle
- Loggerhead

CR
Critically Endangered

A species with an extremely high risk of extinction

- Hawksbill
- Kemp's ridley

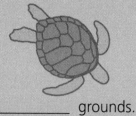

Think and Solve
Study the infographic. Answer the questions.

1. Sea turtles migrate between _____ grounds and _____ grounds.

2. Why do you think that the boxes on the right side of the infographic are colored
the way they are?

_____

_____

3. Does a critically endangered or an endangered species have a greater risk of extinction?

_____

4. Out of every _____ sea turtle eggs, only about one turtle will survive until maturity.

Do the Math
Solve the problems. Use the infographic to help you.

1. For what fraction of an hour can some turtles hold their breath?

_____

2. For every 10,000 eggs laid, about how many sea turtles will survive to adulthood?

_____

3. In 2013, there were about 25,000 green sea turtle nests on Florida beaches. In the box below,
represent the number 25,000 using a pictograph with a key, a model showing ten thousands
and thousands, a multiplication problem, or some other method.

The Visual Guide to Third Grade

Read About It: Pandas in Danger

PANDAS ARE AMONG THE WORLD'S MOST-LOVED FURRY CREATURES. These roly-poly bears are found in the wild only in China. There are less than 2,000 left in the wild, but many groups are working to change this.

The main problem is that the pandas' habitat is being destroyed. As the number of people in China grows, there is less living space for pandas. They eat between 20 and 40 pounds of bamboo a day. As more land is developed, pandas are also losing their main food source.

Pandas do not reproduce often. In fact, females can become pregnant only during two to three days each year. Because pandas have so few cubs, their numbers grow slowly.

Wildlife scientists are working hard to help protect pandas. Keeping their habitat safe is an important step. Researchers are also studying pandas' breeding habits. They hope to find ways to help the population grow faster. Humans are determined not to let these lovable bears ever become extinct!

Compare Information
Fill in the chart using information from the passage above.

PANDA FACTS

Where do they live?	
How many are left in the wild?	
Why are they threatened?	
What do they eat?	
How can they be protected?	

List three ways in which sea turtles and pandas are alike.

_____

_____

_____

Counting Calories

calorie (cal.) = a measurement of the amount of energy a food provides your body with

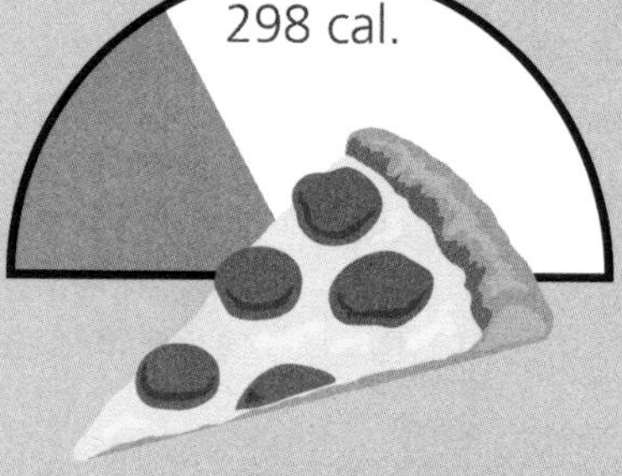

298 cal.

pepperoni pizza (1 slice)

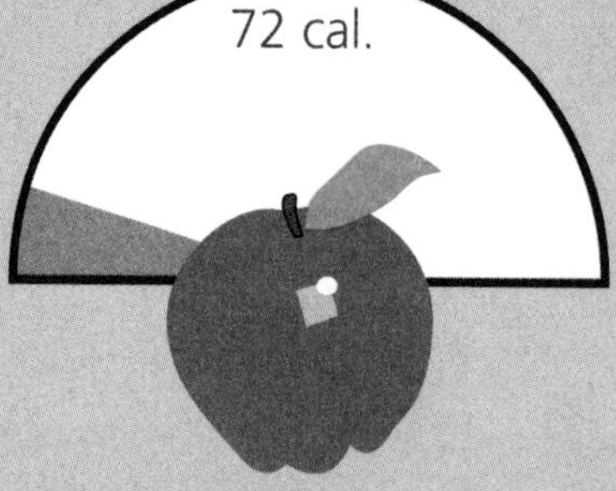

72 cal.

apple

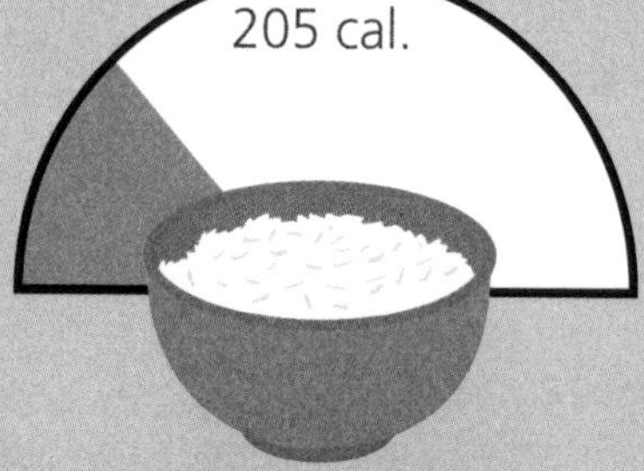

205 cal.

white rice (1 cup)

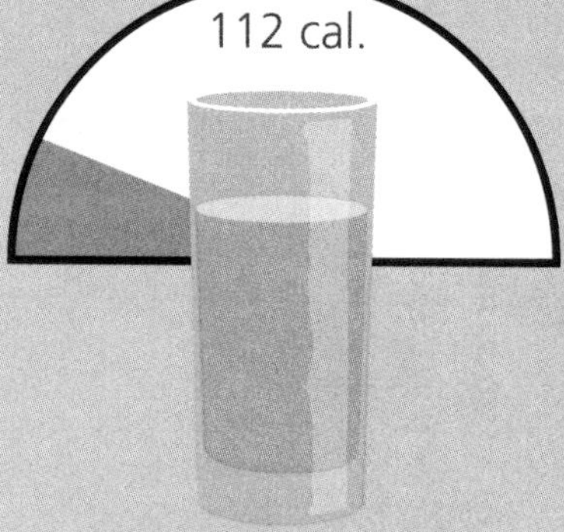

112 cal.

orange juice (8 oz.)

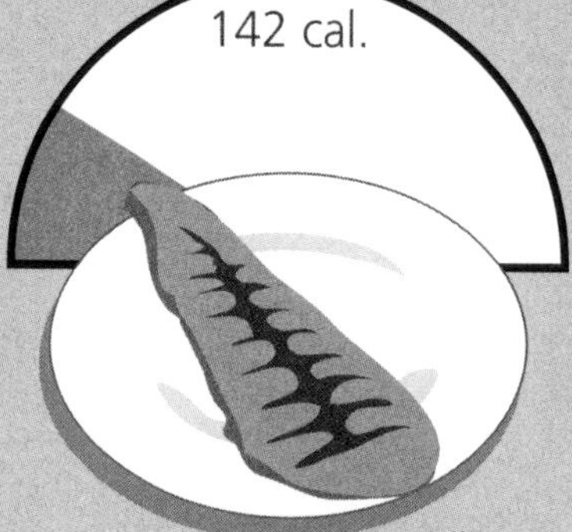

142 cal.

chicken breast (3 oz.)

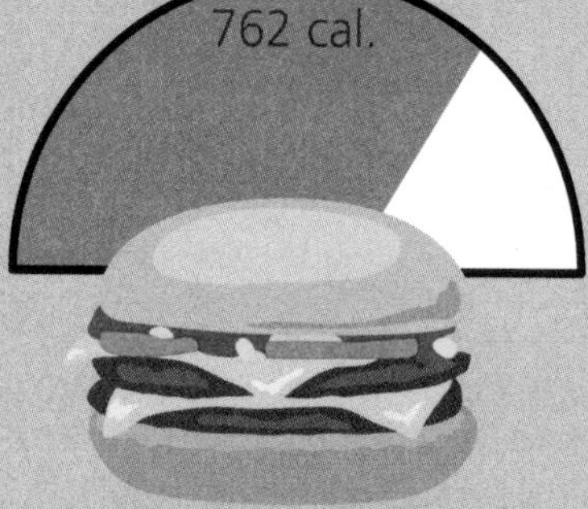

762 cal.

fast-food double cheeseburger

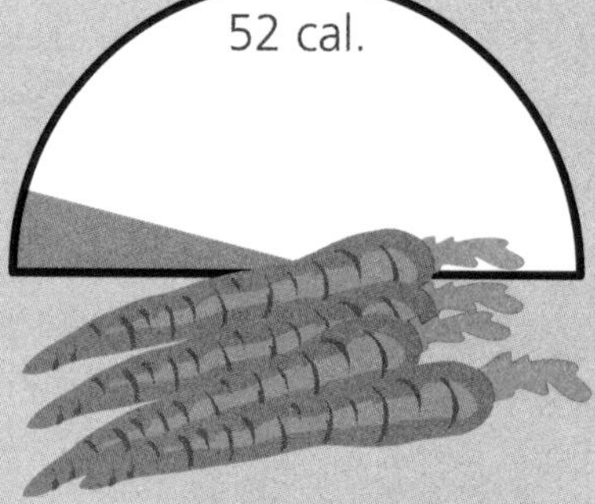

52 cal.

carrots (1 cup)

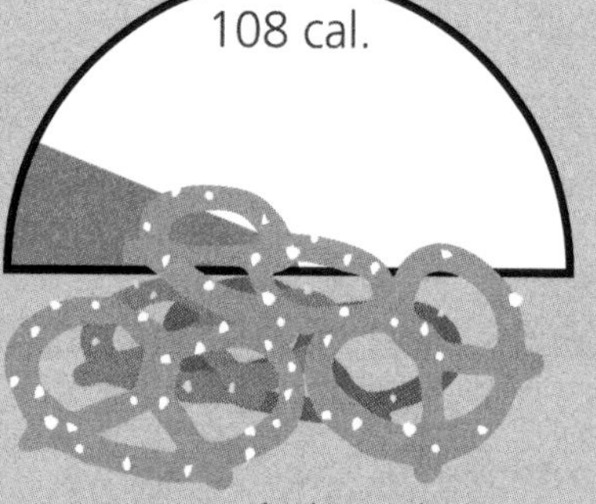

108 cal.

pretzels (1 oz.)

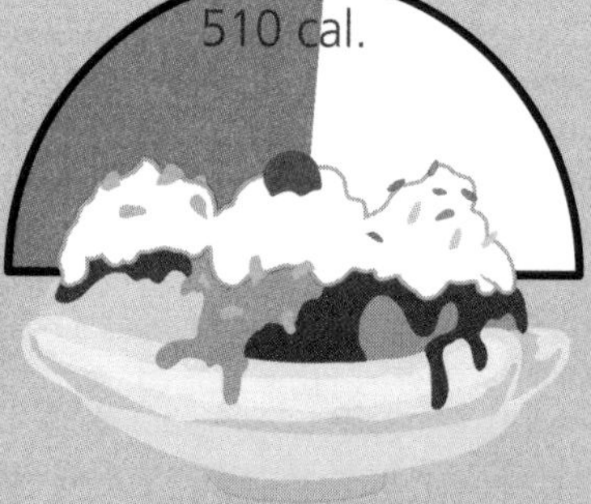

510 cal.

banana split

What's in One Cup?

One cup of different foods can have very different calorie counts!

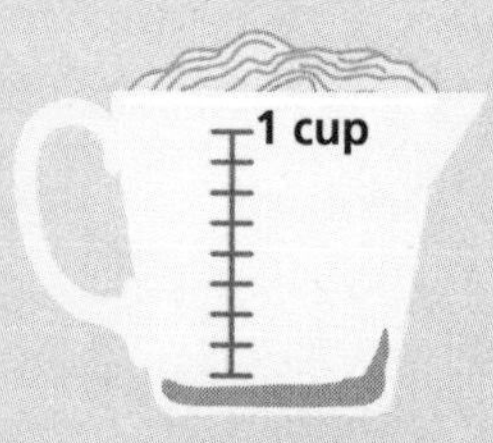

1 cup

spaghetti

221 cal.

1 cup

lettuce

8 cal.

1 cup

canned peaches

109 cal.

1 cup

plain oatmeal

147 cal.

1 cup

ice cream

300 cal.

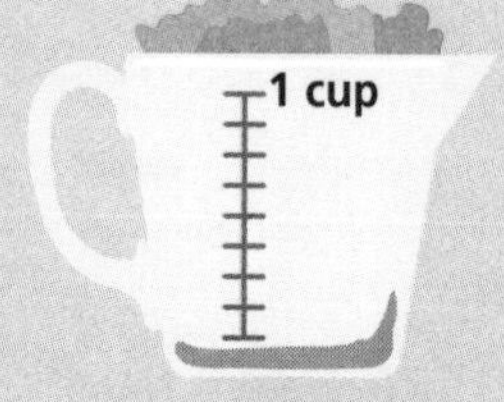

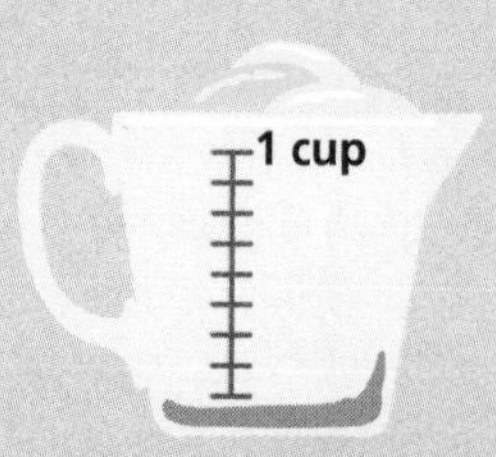

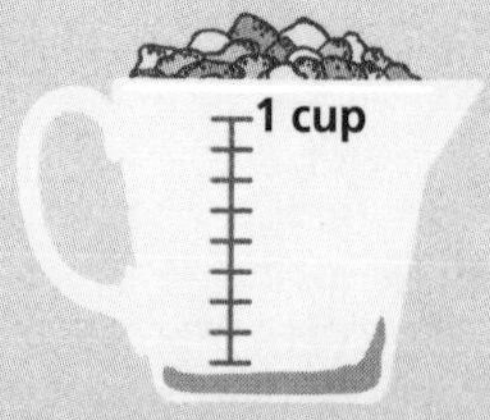

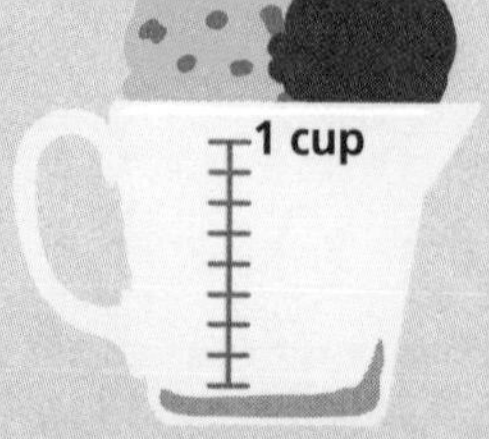

Piece It Together

How many calories do you consume each day? Keep track for one day. Cut out the labels. When you eat one of the foods shown, glue or tape the label into the food log on page 121. If you eat a food that is not shown, create a label for it using one of the blanks. Ask an adult to help you use an online source to find calorie information for each item you add to a blank label.

Cup of Yogurt	Granola Bar	Apple	Egg	Small Salad
90 Calories	150 Calories	70 Calories	90 Calories	60 Calories
Banana	Milk	Chicken Noodle Soup	Cookie	Orange Juice
100 Calories	100 Calories	60 Calories	80 Calories	110 Calories
Peanut Butter Sandwich	Pepperoni Pizza	Broccoli With Butter	Cheeseburger	Chicken Nuggets
320 Calories	300 Calories	65 Calories	300 calories	275 calories
Carrots With Butter	Cornflakes With Milk	Chicken Drumstick	Pretzels	Macaroni and Cheese
80 calories	150 calories	265 calories	100 calories	210 calories

Food: _____   Food: _____   Food: _____   Food: _____   Food: _____

Calories: _____   Calories: _____   Calories: _____   Calories: _____   Calories: _____

Food Log

BREAKFAST

SNACK

LUNCH

SNACK

DINNER

Add up all of the calories shown on the food labels.

How many calories did you eat in one day?_____

Olympic Locations

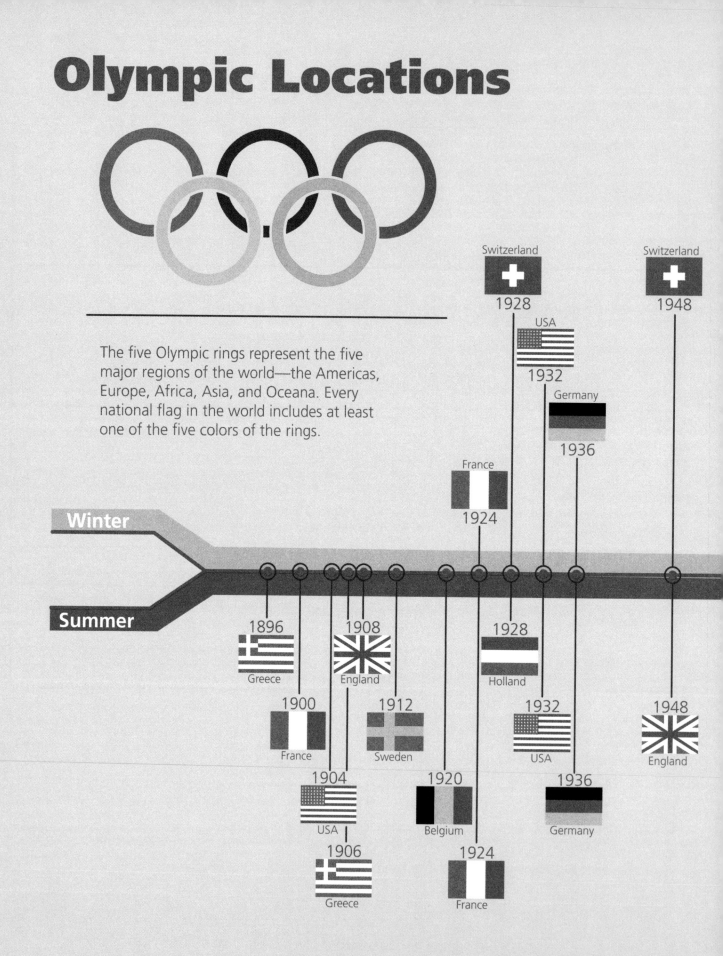

The five Olympic rings represent the five major regions of the world—the Americas, Europe, Africa, Asia, and Oceana. Every national flag in the world includes at least one of the five colors of the rings.

Winter

Summer

Switzerland
1928

Switzerland
1948

USA
1932

Germany
1936

France
1924

1896
Greece

1908
England

1928
Holland

1948
England

1900
France

1912
Sweden

1932
USA

1904
USA

1920
Belgium

1936
Germany

1906
Greece

1924
France

Eight countries
have hosted the
Olympics three
or more times.

Canada ⭕⭕⭕
England ⭕⭕⭕
France ⭕⭕⭕⭕⭕
Germany ⭕⭕⭕

Greece ⭕⭕⭕
Italy ⭕⭕⭕
Japan ⭕⭕⭕
USA ⭕⭕⭕⭕⭕⭕⭕⭕

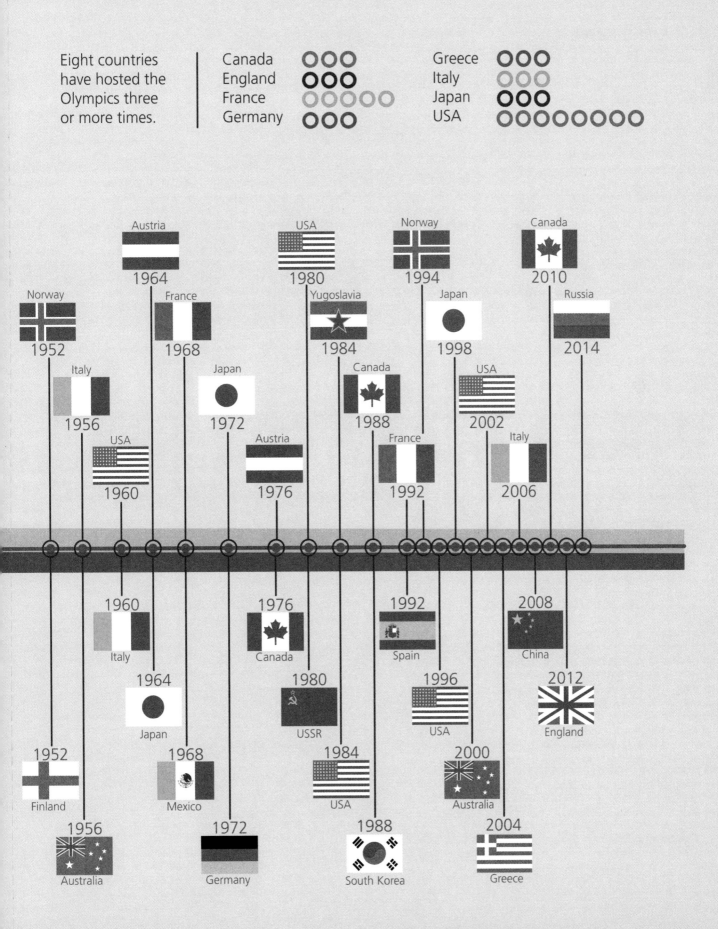

* The Olympic games were canceled in
1916, 1940, and 1944 because of war.

Think and Solve

Study the infographic. Answer the questions.

1. The first summer Olympics were held in Greece in the year _____.

2. How are the flags of Sweden and Finland similar and different?

_____

_____

3. Why were the Olympics canceled in 1916, 1940, and 1944?

_____

4. True or false? France and Germany have each hosted the Olympics two times.

_____

Categorize It

Read the list of Olympic events. Write each event under the correct category.

tennis	fencing	sailing	biathlon
diving	golf	alpine skiing	volleyball
snowboarding	figure skating	ice hockey	rowing
football	judo	triathlon	taekwondo
swimming	pentathlon	basketball	

Events That Use a Ball

_____   _____

_____   _____

_____

Martial Arts

_____   _____

_____

Events That Take Place in the Water

_____   _____

_____   _____

Events That Take Place on Ice or Snow

_____   _____

_____   _____

Events That Involve More Than One Sport

_____   _____   _____

Map It

This map shows the continents of the world. Use the infographic to make a tally mark on a continent each time a country on that continent has hosted the Olympics. If you are not sure on what continent a country is found, use a globe, an atlas, or an online map to look it up. (Note: The country of Russia was once known as the USSR. It spans two continents. Count it in both.)

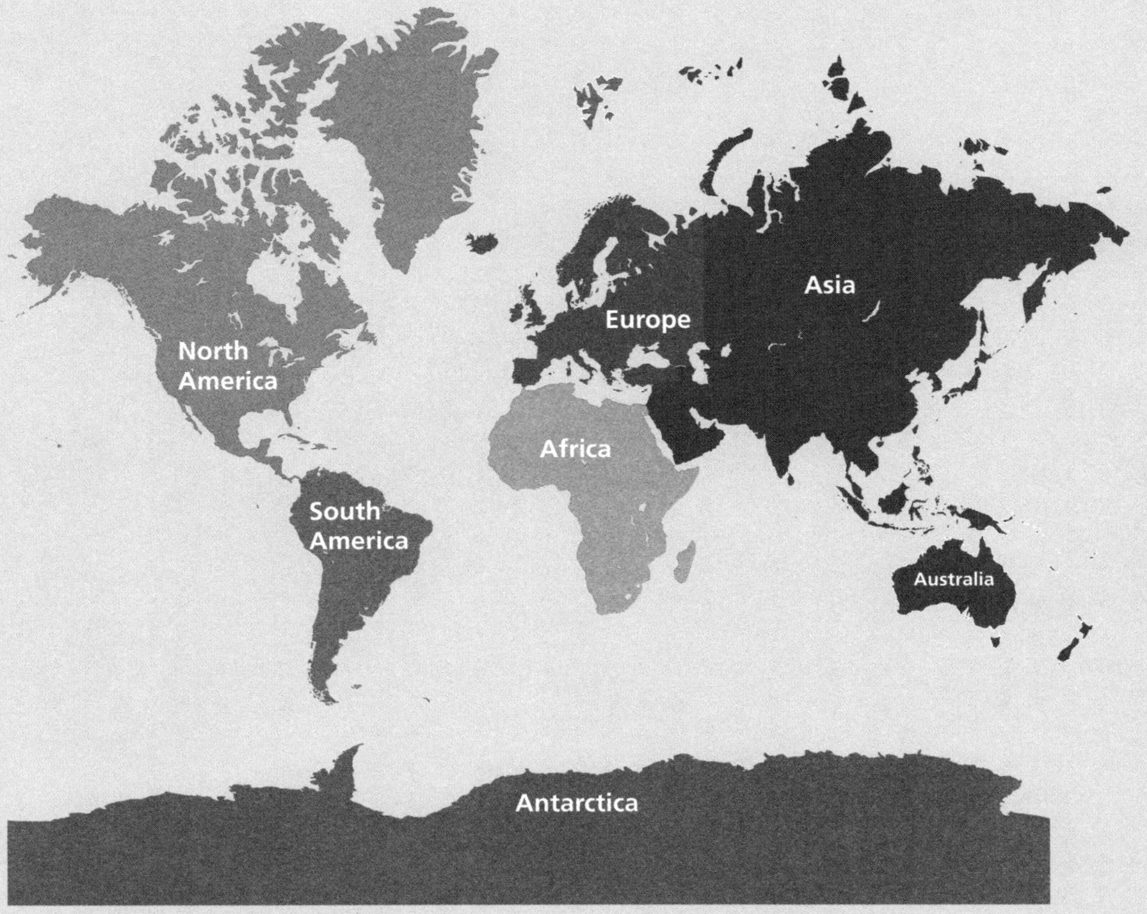

Asia

Australia

Europe

Africa

North America

South America

Antarctica

Now, count your tally marks.
How many times have the Olympic
Games been held on each continent?

Africa: _____

Antarctica: _____

Asia: _____

Australia: _____

Europe: _____

North America: _____

South America: _____

Amelia Earhart: Soaring Into History

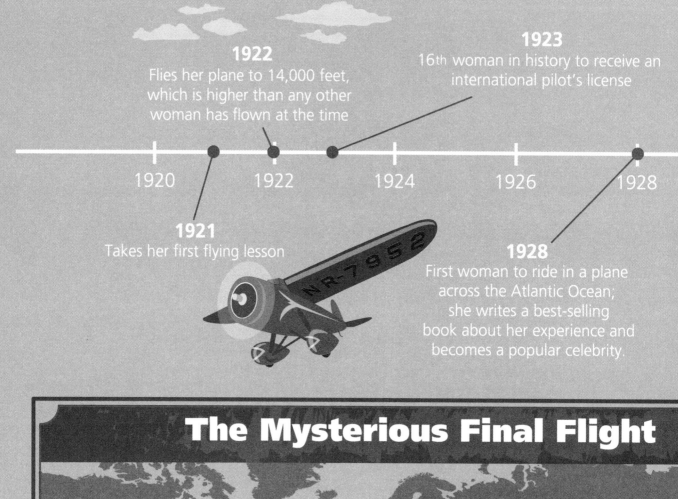

1922
Flies her plane to 14,000 feet, which is higher than any other woman has flown at the time

1923
16th woman in history to receive an international pilot's license

1920 1922 1924 1926 1928

1921
Takes her first flying lesson

1928
First woman to ride in a plane across the Atlantic Ocean; she writes a best-selling book about her experience and becomes a popular celebrity.

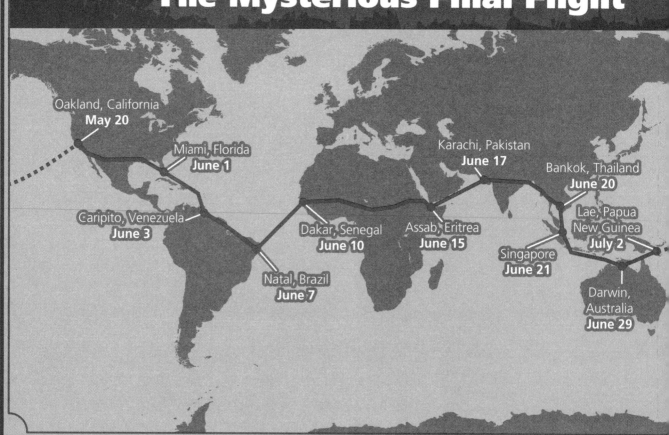

The Mysterious Final Flight

Oakland, California
May 20

Miami, Florida
June 1

Caripito, Venezuela
June 3

Dakar, Senegal
June 10

Natal, Brazil
June 7

Assab, Eritrea
June 15

Karachi, Pakistan
June 17

Bankok, Thailand
June 20

Singapore
June 21

Lae, Papua New Guinea
July 2

Darwin, Australia
June 29

1930
Sets the women's world flying speed record when she flies more than 180 miles per hour

180

1935
First person to fly solo from Hawaii to California

1930   1932   1934   1936   1938

1932
First woman to fly solo, or alone, across the Atlantic Ocean
Three months later, she is the first woman to fly solo and nonstop from coast to coast across America.

1937
On June 1, she sets out to fly around the world. She and her navigator, Fred Noonan, complete nearly 22,000 miles of the journey. On July 2, they disappear somewhere in the middle of the Pacific Ocean.

Some believed Amelia was a spy, but this has never been proven. Her body and plane have never been found. Her disappearance is one of the most enduring mysteries of the 20th century.

Before vanishing, Amelia sent radio messages to a Coast Guard ship.

First message: *"plane is low on gas, visibility is poor"*
Final message: Received July 2, 1937 at 8:44 A.M.
"We are on the line of position 157-337…will repeat this message. We are running north and south."

Amelia was never heard from again.

The Search:
- Ordered by the president of the United States
- Cost over 4 million dollars
- Lasted 2 weeks
- Covered 250,000 square miles (647,497 sq. km) of sea
- No clues were found

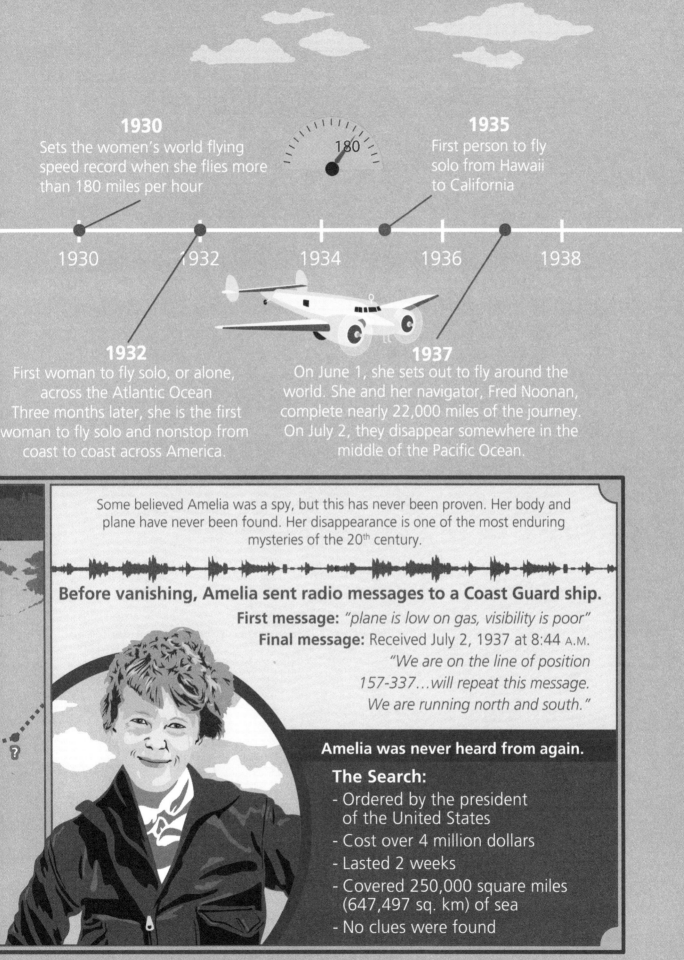

Think and Solve

Study the infographic. Answer the questions.

1. One mile is equal to 5,280 feet. Measured in miles, about how high did Amelia Earhart fly when she set her record for flying height in 1922?

    A. 1 mile

    B. $2\frac{1}{2}$ miles

    C. 3 miles

    D. $4\frac{1}{2}$ miles

2. The search for Amelia covered 250,000 square miles. Why did it cover such a large area?

_____

3. List three countries Amelia Earhart flew over during her attempt to circle the globe.

_____   _____   _____

4. True or false? Amelia Earhart was the first woman to receive an international pilot's license.

_____

5. How many years passed between Amelia's first flying lesson and her disappearance?

_____

6. How many miles of Amelia's total journey were not completed? Use the pictograph below to answer. _____

Amelia's Final Flight

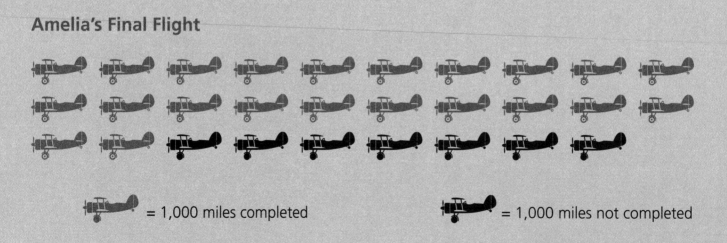

= 1,000 miles completed   = 1,000 miles not completed

Write About It

An *obituary* is an article about a person who died recently. The article usually tells interesting or important facts about the person's life, including the reason he or she died. Under the newspaper headline below, write an obituary for Amelia Earhart. Use information from the infographic.

DAILY NEWS

SEARCH ENDS FOR EARHART'S PLANE

Amelia Earhart

The Buzz on Honeybees

In the 1940s, there were 5 million honeybee colonies. Today, the number has decreased by half to only 2.5 million.

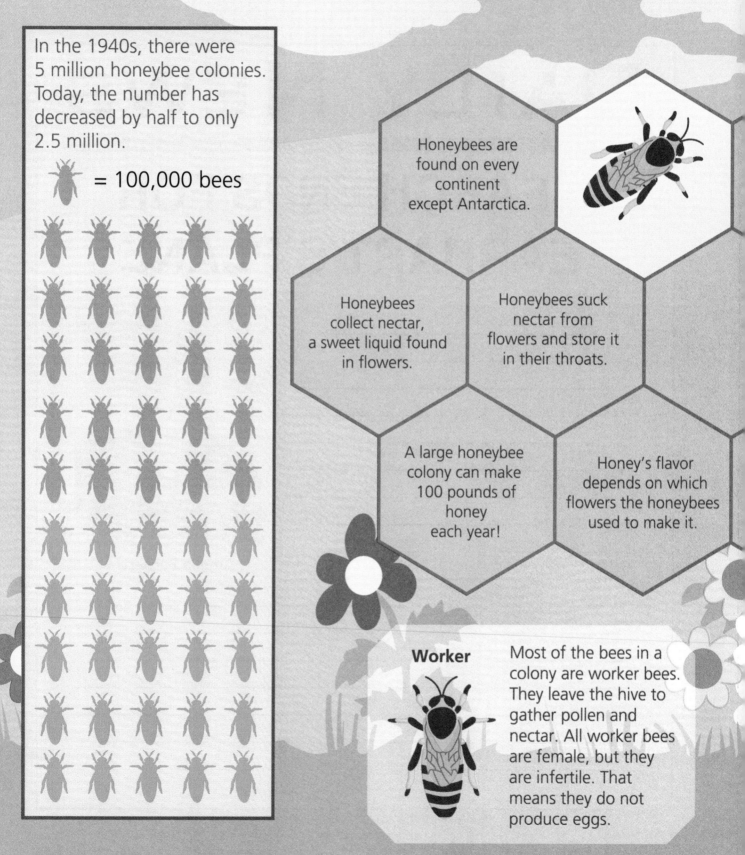

= 100,000 bees

Honeybees are found on every continent except Antarctica.

Honeybees collect nectar, a sweet liquid found in flowers.

Honeybees suck nectar from flowers and store it in their throats.

A large honeybee colony can make 100 pounds of honey each year!

Honey's flavor depends on which flowers the honeybees used to make it.

Worker

Most of the bees in a colony are worker bees. They leave the hive to gather pollen and nectar. All worker bees are female, but they are infertile. That means they do not produce eggs.

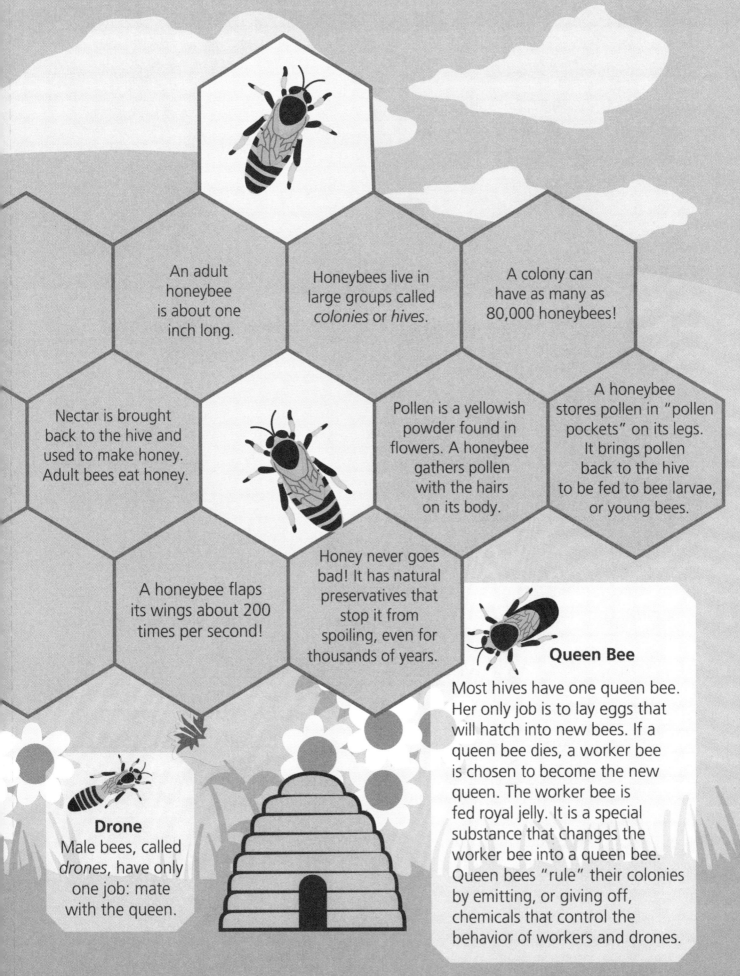

An adult honeybee is about one inch long.

Honeybees live in large groups called *colonies* or *hives*.

A colony can have as many as 80,000 honeybees!

Nectar is brought back to the hive and used to make honey. Adult bees eat honey.

Pollen is a yellowish powder found in flowers. A honeybee gathers pollen with the hairs on its body.

A honeybee stores pollen in "pollen pockets" on its legs. It brings pollen back to the hive to be fed to bee larvae, or young bees.

A honeybee flaps its wings about 200 times per second!

Honey never goes bad! It has natural preservatives that stop it from spoiling, even for thousands of years.

Queen Bee

Most hives have one queen bee. Her only job is to lay eggs that will hatch into new bees. If a queen bee dies, a worker bee is chosen to become the new queen. The worker bee is fed royal jelly. It is a special substance that changes the worker bee into a queen bee. Queen bees "rule" their colonies by emitting, or giving off, chemicals that control the behavior of workers and drones.

Drone
Male bees, called *drones*, have only one job: mate with the queen.

Think and Solve
Study the infographic. Answer the questions.

1. What do adult honeybees eat?

    A. pollen   **C.** nectar

    B. honey   **D.** The infographic does not have this information.

2. True or false? Honey that was made hundreds of years ago can still be eaten.

_____

3. When would a worker bee be fed royal jelly?

_____

4. What is a drone?

    A. a worker bee   **C.** a young bee

    B. a queen bee that has been fed royal jelly   **D.** a male bee

5. What are pollen pockets?

_____

_____

Do the Math
Solve the problems. Use the infographic to help you.

1. A honeybee hovers in the air for 8 seconds. About how many times does it flap its wings?

_____

2. Which expression shows how many fewer honeybee colonies there are today than in the 1940s?

    A. $5,000,000 \times 2$ **C.** $5,000,000 - \frac{1}{2}$

    B. $5,000,000 \div 2$ **D.** $5,000,000 + \frac{1}{2}$

3. A queen bee lays around 1,500 eggs per day. How many eggs does she lay in a week?

_____

4. A hive produces 30 pounds of honey. The beekeeper takes 25 pounds of honey to sell. Which fraction shows how much of the total honey is taken by the beekeeper?

    A. $\frac{6}{5}$ **C.** $\frac{2}{3}$

    B. $\frac{5}{6}$ **D.** $\frac{30}{25}$

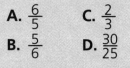

Write About It

Imagine you are a honeybee. What do you do all day? On the lines below, write a diary entry describing a day in your life.

Levitating Trains

Maglev trains are magnetic levitation trains used for transportation across large distances. They were first imagined in the early 1900s, but have only been in commercial use since 1984 and in public use since the early 2000s.

OVER 372 MPH

Maglev trains can travel more than 372 mph (600 kmh) because the traditional source of friction between the track and wheels is eliminated. Maglev trains generally travel at a speed of 267 mph (430 kmh).

DECEMBER 2003

First public commercial maglev trip happened in Shanghai, China

BETWEEN 1 TO 10 CM

of distance between the train and the track

1 cm

10 cm

40 MINUTES

to make a 174-mile (280 km) trip

$100 BILLION

to build a 178-mile (286 km) maglev rail in Japan between Tokyo and Nagoya by 2027

Opposites Attract

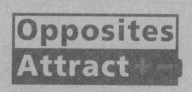

Maglev trains can levitate due to magnetic forces. The trains use electromagnets to suspend and propel the train forward.

Piece It Together

The pictures below show different forms of transportation and the average speed of each in miles per hour. Cut out each form of transportation and glue or tape it above the correct speed in the graph on page 137.

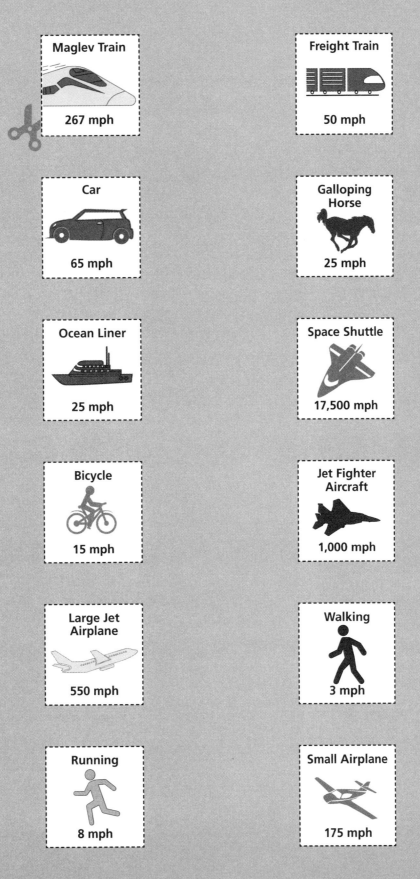

Maglev Train 267 mph	**Freight Train** 50 mph
Car 65 mph	**Galloping Horse** 25 mph
Ocean Liner 25 mph	**Space Shuttle** 17,500 mph
Bicycle 15 mph	**Jet Fighter Aircraft** 1,000 mph
Large Jet Airplane 550 mph	**Walking** 3 mph
Running 8 mph	**Small Airplane** 175 mph

Speed Graph

One form of transportation does not fit on the graph. Put it here:

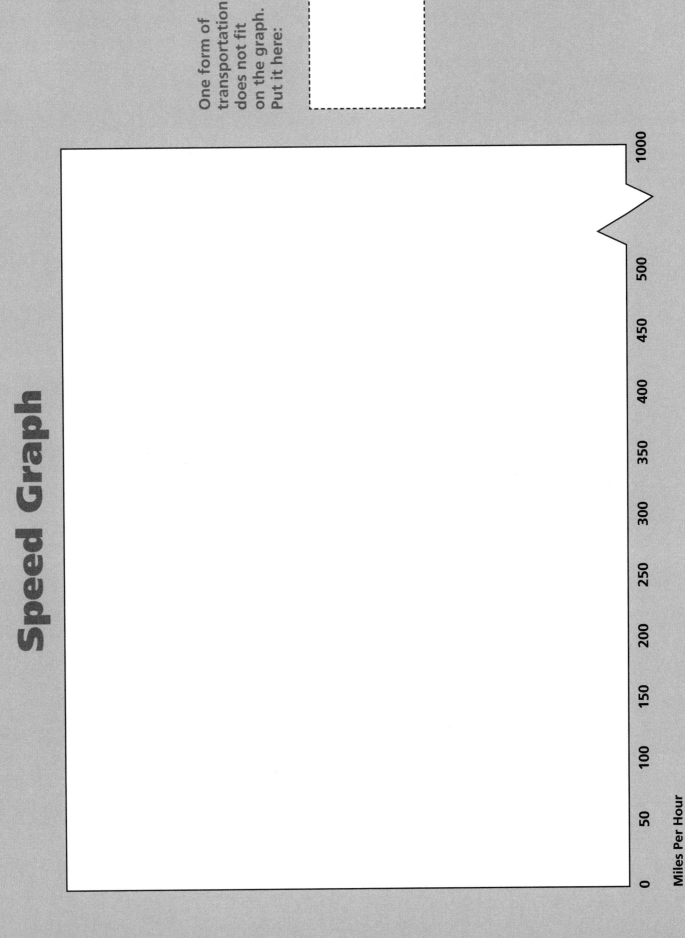

Miles Per Hour

0   50   100   150   200   250   300   350   400   450   500   1000

Solar System Statistics

This illustration shows the sizes of the planets compared to each other. It also shows an everyday object of the same size as each planet if the Sun were the size of standard 8-inch playground ball.*

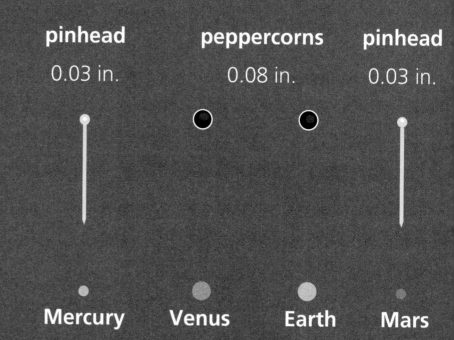

pinhead
0.03 in.

peppercorns
0.08 in.

pinhead
0.03 in.

Mercury   **Venus**   **Earth**   **Mars**

playground ball
8 in.

MERCURY orbits the Sun faster than any other planet. It takes only 88 Earth days!

VENUS is the easiest planet to see from Earth. In fact, it is the third brightest object in the sky after the Sun and the Moon.

EARTH is the only planet where water is found in all three states: solid (ice), liquid (water), and gas (water vapor).

The tallest mountain in the solar system is a volcano on **MARS** called *Olympus Mons*. It is almost three times as tall as Mount Everest!

JUPITER has 62 known moons. The largest, Ganymede, is the biggest moon in the solar system. It is bigger than the planet Mercury!

SATURN'S rings are made of ice and dust. Although they stretch out into space for about 282,000 km, they are only about 1 km thick.

URANUS is the coldest planet in the solar system. Temperatures can reach –224°C.

NEPTUNE orbits the Sun once every 164 Earth years. It has completed only one orbit since its discovery in 1846.

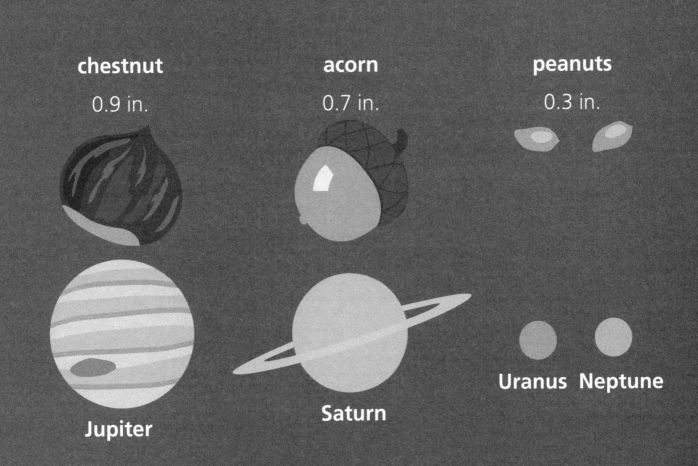

chestnut
0.9 in.

acorn
0.7 in.

peanuts
0.3 in.

Jupiter

Saturn

Uranus Neptune

Planet	Diameter (rounded to nearest 100 km)	Distance From the Sun (rounded to nearest 1,000,000 km)
Mercury	4,900 km	58,000,000 km
Venus	12,100 km	108,000,000 km
Earth	12,800 km	150,000,000 km
Mars	6,800 km	228,000,000 km
Jupiter	143,000 km	778,000,000 km
Saturn	120,500 km	1,429,000,000 km
Uranus	51,100 km	2,871,000,000 km
Neptune	49,500 km	4,500,000,000 km

*The distances between the planets and the Sun are not to scale.

Think and Solve
Study the infographic. Answer the questions.

1. True or false? The infographic shows a peanut for the sizes of Uranus and Neptune because those planets are about the same size.

   _____

2. What is Ganymede?

   A. the largest moon in the solar system

   B. another name for Jupiter

   C. the tallest mountain in the solar system

   D. the brightest object in the sky

3. Which planet orbits the Sun in the shortest amount of time?

   _____

Do the Math
Solve the problems. Use the infographic to help you.

1. What is the distance between Earth and Saturn?

   _____

2. True or false? Neptune is about three times farther from the Sun than Saturn.

   _____

3. During a single Earth year, Mercury orbits the sun about _____times.

   A. 2   **C.** 4

   B. 3   **D.** 5

4. Neptune is about _____kilometers from the Sun.

   A. four million, five hundred thousand

   B. forty-five million

   C. four hundred fifty million

   D. four billion, five hundred million

5. The diameter of the largest planet, Jupiter, is about _____times bigger than the diameter of the smallest planet, Mercury.

   A. 20   **C.** 40

   B. 29   **D.** 99

Label It

Someone forgot to label the planets shown below. They are arranged in order of size, not distance from the Sun. Using information from the infographic, label each planet with its name and its diameter in kilometers. Then, color the planets.

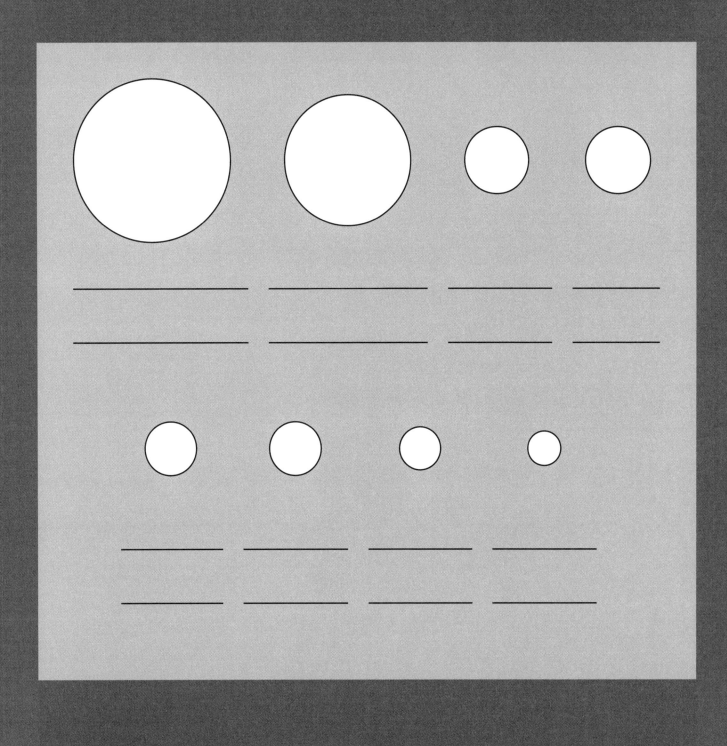

Hurricanes vs. Tornadoes

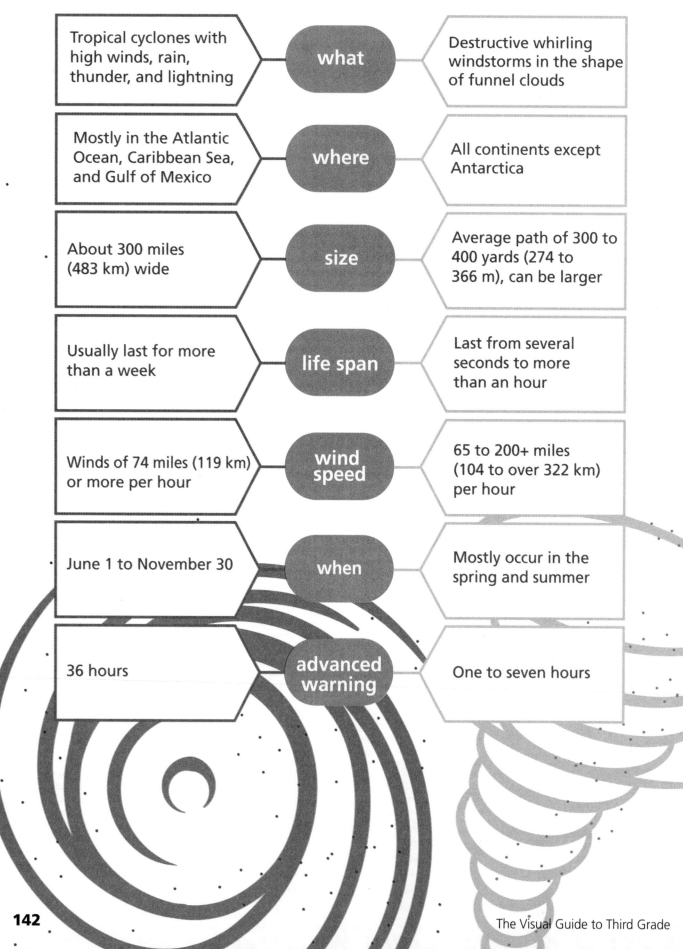

Hurricanes		Tornadoes
Tropical cyclones with high winds, rain, thunder, and lightning	**what**	Destructive whirling windstorms in the shape of funnel clouds
Mostly in the Atlantic Ocean, Caribbean Sea, and Gulf of Mexico	**where**	All continents except Antarctica
About 300 miles (483 km) wide	**size**	Average path of 300 to 400 yards (274 to 366 m), can be larger
Usually last for more than a week	**life span**	Last from several seconds to more than an hour
Winds of 74 miles (119 km) or more per hour	**wind speed**	65 to 200+ miles (104 to over 322 km) per hour
June 1 to November 30	**when**	Mostly occur in the spring and summer
36 hours	**advanced warning**	One to seven hours

Think and Solve

Study the infographic. Answer the questions.

1. True or false? Some tornadoes last for only a few seconds.

_____

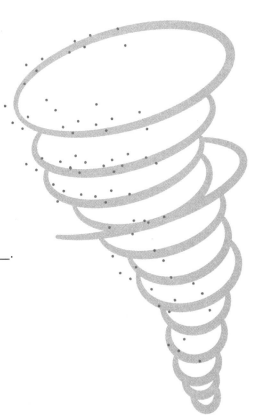

2. Which is not a place where hurricanes are likely to occur?

    A. Hudson Bay

    B. Caribbean Sea

    C. Gulf of Mexico

    D. Atlantic Ocean

3. Hurricane season lasts for about _____.

    A. $\frac{1}{6}$ of the year

    B. $\frac{1}{4}$ of the year

    C. $\frac{1}{3}$ of the year

    D. $\frac{1}{2}$ of the year

4. Tornadoes occur on every continent except _____.

5. Explain what a tornado looks like.

_____

_____

6. Which storm can have the highest wind speeds?

_____

7. Do you think it is easier to avoid a hurricane or a tornado? Why?

_____

_____

8. True or false? An average hurricane measures about 300 yards across.

_____

The Wright Brothers

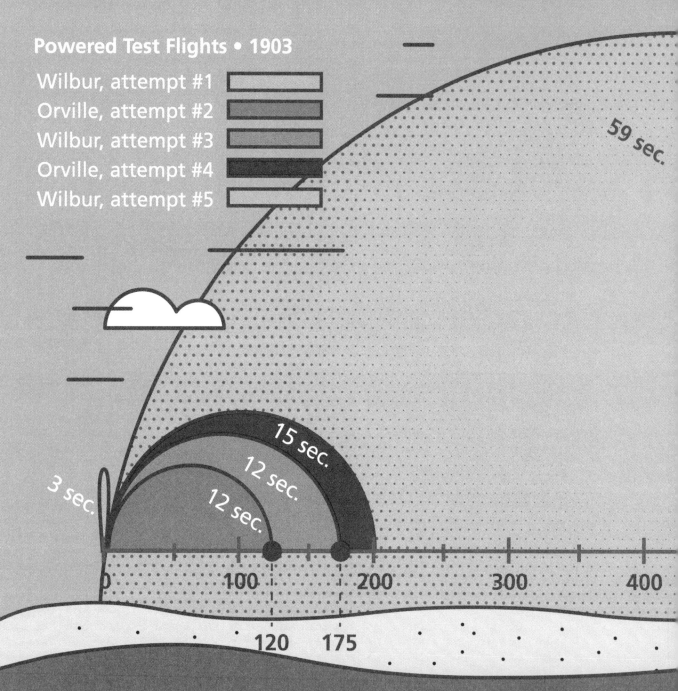

Powered Test Flights • 1903

Wilbur, attempt #1
Orville, attempt #2
Wilbur, attempt #3
Orville, attempt #4
Wilbur, attempt #5

59 sec.

15 sec.

12 sec.

12 sec.

3 sec.

0   100   200   300   400

120   175

The Wright brothers, Orville and Wilbur, were two American inventors and aviation pioneers who invented and built the world's first successful airplane. The airplane was actually a glider with wheels and an engine. The brothers chose a beach near Kitty Hawk, North Carolina, as the place to test their new invention. They needed a place with lots of wind, in case the engine on their glider failed.

On December 14, 1903, Wilbur Wright made the first attempt with a man-powered airplane flight. The brothers tossed a coin to see who would go first and Wilbur won. Unfortunately, the flight only lasted a little more than three seconds and ended with a crash!

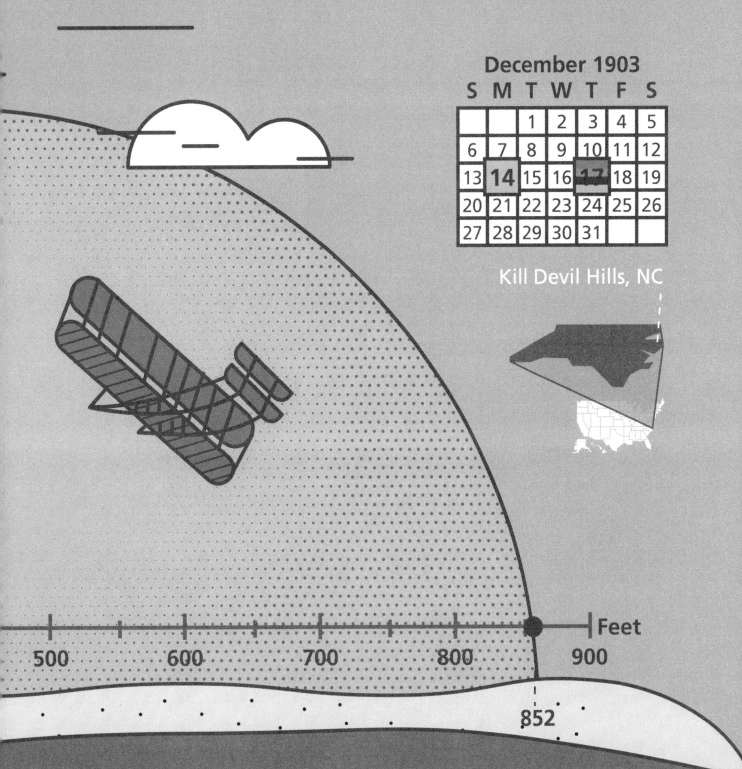

December 1903

S	M	T	W	T	F	S
		1	2	3	4	5
6	7	8	9	10	11	12
13	**14**	15	16	17	18	19
20	21	22	23	24	25	26
27	28	29	30	31		

Kill Devil Hills, NC

500   600   700   800   Feet   900

852

With a repaired airplane, the brothers were ready to try again on December 17. This time, it was Orville's turn to fly the plane. The first try that day resulted in only a 12-second flight. The airplane landed only 120 feet from where it first took off. But, it was officially the first time a human had ever flown! The Wright brothers made three more flights that day with each brother taking a turn flying the plane. The most significant flight was the last one. Wilbur flew the airplane 852 feet, staying in the air for almost one full minute.

Think and Solve
Study the infographic. Answer the questions.

1. Why did the Wright brothers choose Kitty Hawk, North Carolina, as the place to test
their airplane?

_____

2. True or false? Wilbur flew the plane for each attempt while Orville timed the flights.

_____

3. What do you predict would have happened if there had been another test flight on December 17th?

_____

Do the Math
Solve the problems. Use the infographic to help you.

1. What was the speed of the first flight on December 17?

   A. 10 feet per second

   B. 20 feet per second

   C. 30 feet per second

   D. 40 feet per second

2. How much farther did the plane fly on the final attempt than on the fourth attempt?

_____

3. In the third attempt, the plane flew _____ farther than in the second attempt.

   A. 52 feet

   B. 45 feet

   C. 10 feet

   D. 55 feet

4. How many years ago did the Wright brothers fly their plane at Kitty Hawk?

_____

5. What was the average distance the Wright brothers flew in their four attempts on December 17?
Round your answer to the nearest whole number.

   A. 25 feet

   B. 165 feet

   C. 337 feet

   D. 526 feet

Make a Paper Airplane

Tear this page from the book. Cut along the solid dark line. Then, follow the instructions on page 149 to fold along the dotted lines and create a paper airplane.

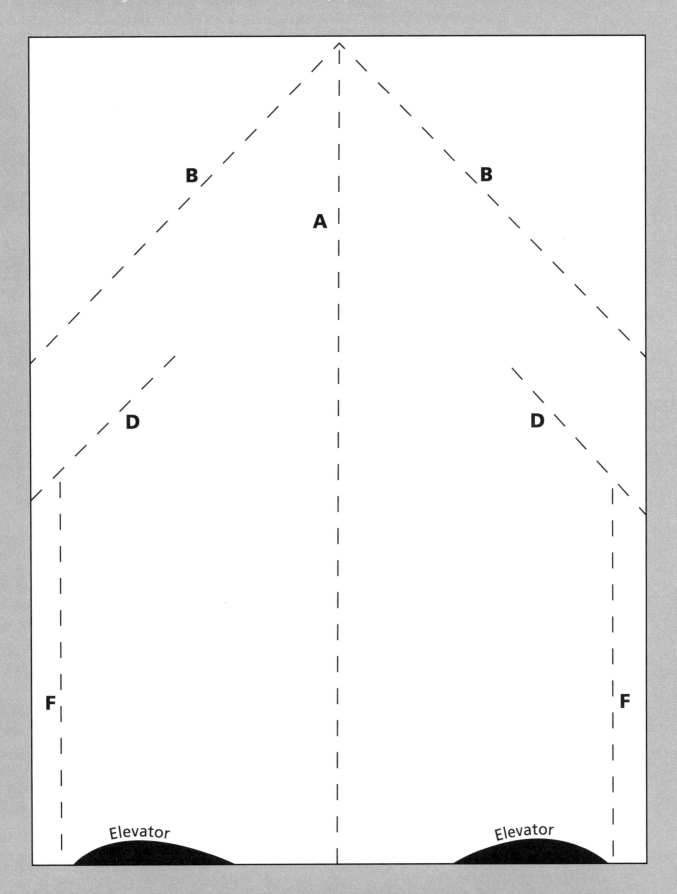

B

A

B

D

D

F

F

Elevator

Elevator

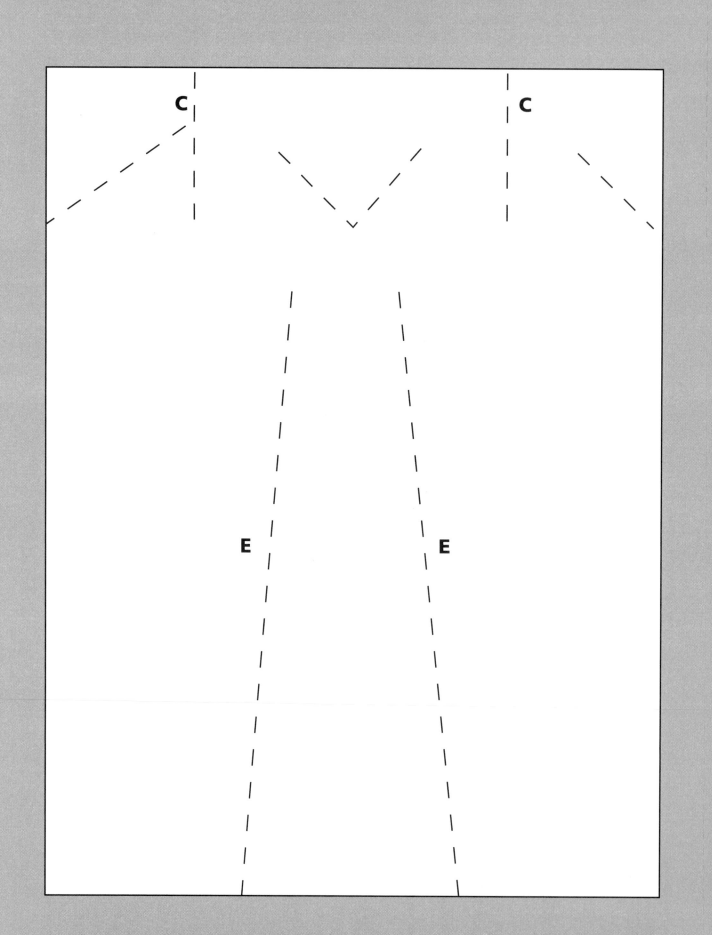

Follow the directions below to fold your paper airplane. As you make each fold, keep the dotted line inside the fold. In other words, once you make the fold, you should not see the line.

 1. Fold the paper in half along Line A. Then, unfold it.

 2. Fold along Lines B so the two top corners meet at Line A.

3. Fold along Line C so the top point is down.

4. Fold along Lines D so the paper is shaped like a pentagon.

5. Fold in half along Line A again.

6. Fold down along Lines E to create the wings. Fold up along Lines F to finish the wings.

Collect Data

Now, test your airplane. Try throwing it in different ways. If the plane is flying straight up or down, try bending the elevators up or down to see if that helps.

Fly your plane 10 times. Use a yardstick or measuring tape to record the flight distance each time. Record your data by drawing a bar on the chart to show how far your plane flew each time.

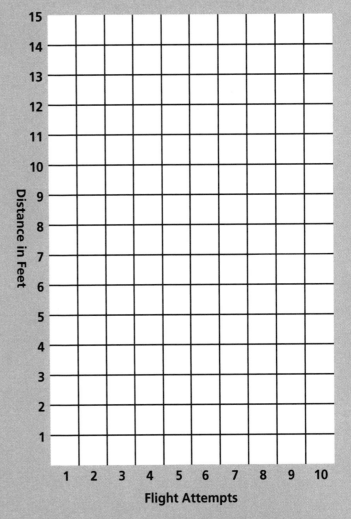

Distance in Feet

15
14
13
12
11
10
9
8
7
6
5
4
3
2
1

1   2   3   4   5   6   7   8   9   10

Flight Attempts

Nature's Doorways

Arches National Park in Utah is home to the most natural stone arches in the world. It also has many other rock formations, such as pinnacles, fins, and balanced rocks. This desert wonderland was formed from a combination of deposition, erosion, and water dissolving and breaking the sandstone from the inside out over millions of years.

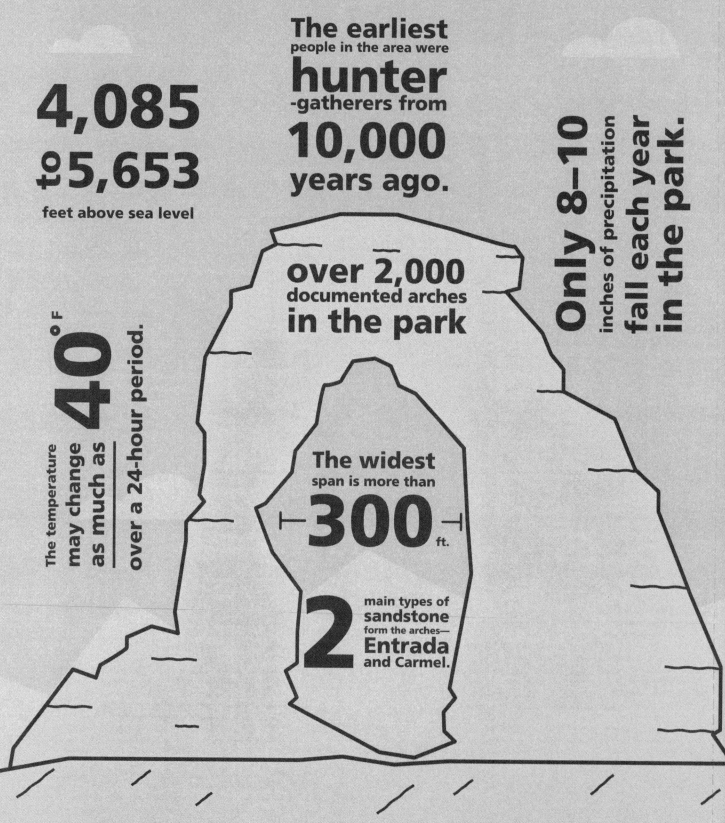

4,085 to 5,653 feet above sea level

The earliest people in the area were **hunter**-gatherers from **10,000** years ago.

Only 8–10 inches of precipitation **fall each year in the park.**

The temperature **may change as much as 40°F** over a 24-hour period.

over 2,000 documented arches **in the park**

The widest span is more than **300** ft.

2 main types of sandstone form the arches— **Entrada** and Carmel.

Think and Solve
Study the infographic. Answer the questions.

1. The rock formations at Arches National Park formed over _____ of years.

   A. hundreds

   B. thousands

   C. millions

   D. billions

2. What are fins and pinnacles?

   _____

3. True or false? All of the arches at the park are made of a type of sandstone called *entrada*.

   _____

4. How did the arches form?

   _____

   _____

Do the Math
Solve the problems. Use the infographic to help you.

1. What is the difference between the highest point at Arches National Park and the lowest point?

   _____ feet

2. How much rain could you expect to fall at Arches National Park during a five-year period?

   about _____ to _____ inches

3. The widest arch spans more than _____ yards across.

4. Delicate Arch is the most famous arch at the park. It is 65 feet tall. The tallest arch at the park is Double Arch. It is 112 feet tall. How much taller is Double Arch than Delicate Arch?

   _____ feet

Fractured Earth

Plates under Earth's surface shift, slide, and collide—causing earthquakes, volcanoes, and giant cracks called *faults*.

San Andreas Fault

The San Andreas Fault is where the eastern edge of the Pacific plate meets the western edge of the North American plate. The Pacific plate is moving very slowly to the northwest. As it scrapes alongside the North American plate, pressure builds up. When the pressure is released, the energy makes the ground shake. That's an earthquake!

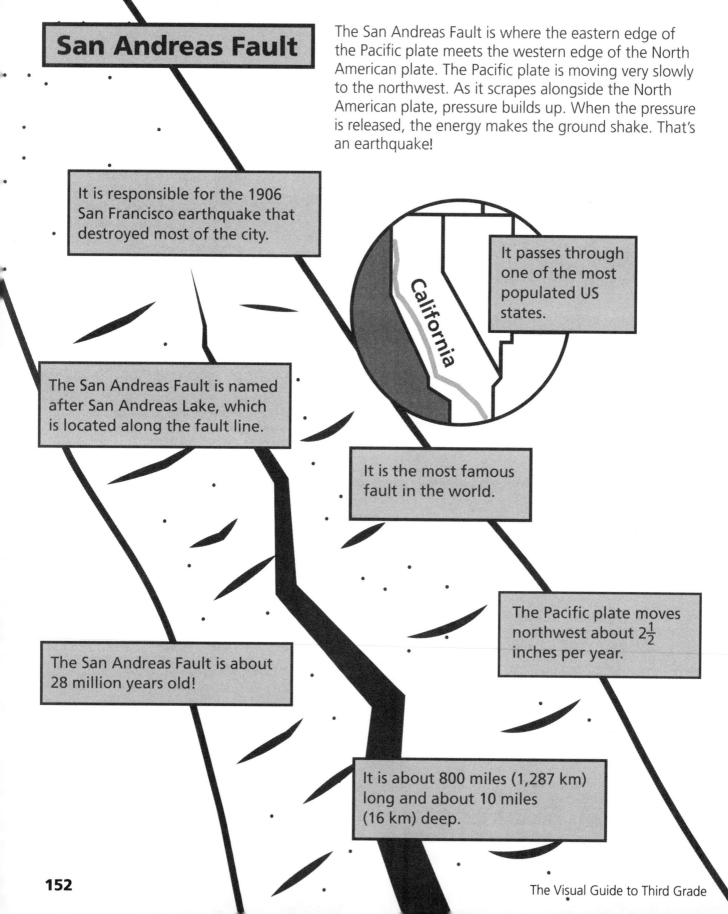

It is responsible for the 1906 San Francisco earthquake that destroyed most of the city.

It passes through one of the most populated US states.

California

The San Andreas Fault is named after San Andreas Lake, which is located along the fault line.

It is the most famous fault in the world.

The Pacific plate moves northwest about $2\frac{1}{2}$ inches per year.

The San Andreas Fault is about 28 million years old!

It is about 800 miles (1,287 km) long and about 10 miles (16 km) deep.

Mariana Trench

The Mariana Trench is where the western edge of the Pacific plate meets the eastern edge of the Philippine plate. Instead of moving alongside each other, the Pacific plate is moving under the Philippine plate. As one plate slopes downward to move under the other, it makes a deep trench in the ocean floor.

Water pressure at the bottom of the trench is enormous: 16,000 pounds per square inch!

Because it lies within US territories, it was named a US national monument in 2009.

The world's strongest earthquakes occur in places like the Mariana Trench, where one plate moves underneath another.

In 1960, Jacques Piccard and Donald Walsh became the first humans to explore the bottom of the trench.

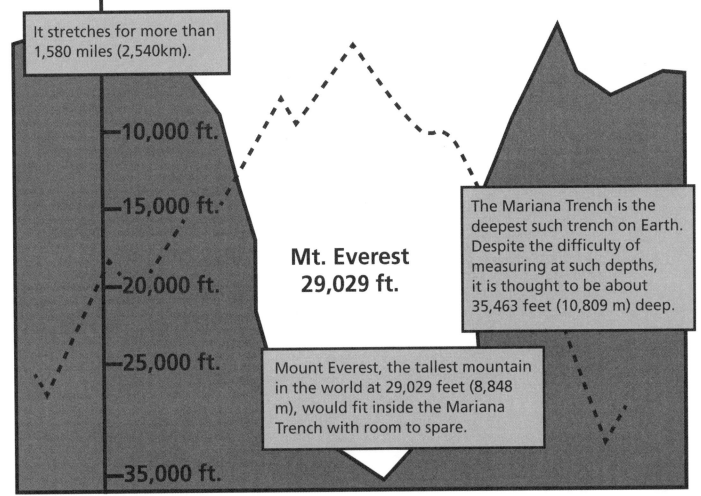

—1,000 ft.

It stretches for more than 1,580 miles (2,540km).

—10,000 ft.

—15,000 ft.

—20,000 ft.

Mt. Everest 29,029 ft.

The Mariana Trench is the deepest such trench on Earth. Despite the difficulty of measuring at such depths, it is thought to be about 35,463 feet (10,809 m) deep.

—25,000 ft.

Mount Everest, the tallest mountain in the world at 29,029 feet (8,848 m), would fit inside the Mariana Trench with room to spare.

—35,000 ft.

Think and Solve

Study the infographic. Answer the questions.

1. True or false? No one has ever visited the deepest parts of the Mariana Trench.

_____

2. The Grand Canyon is 277 miles long. How much longer is the Mariana Trench?

    A. 1,303 miles

    B. 1,000 feet

    C. 3,003 miles

    D. 33,000 feet

3. Which two plates meet to form the San Andreas Fault?

_____ and _____

4. The distance to the bottom of the Mariana Trench is _____

feet longer than the height of Mount Everest.

Compare and Contrast

Complete the Venn diagram to compare the San Andreas Fault and the Mariana Trench. Write facts about each one in the large circles. In the overlapping part, write facts that are true about both. Use the infographic to help you.

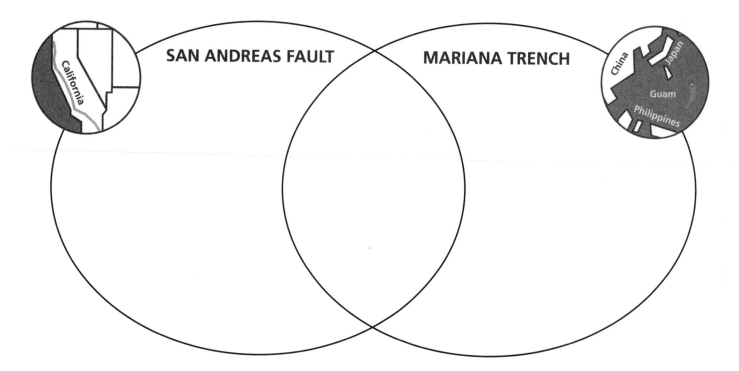

Make a Time Line

Read the list of powerful and memorable earthquakes since 1900. Then, use the time line to show the earthquakes in chronological order. Write the location of each earthquake near the year it happened.

LOCATION	DATE	MAGNITUDE	DESCRIPTION
Chile	5/22/1960	9.5	strongest earthquake ever measured
Alaska	3/27/1964	9.2	strongest US quake ever measured
Indonesia	12/26/2004	9.1	strongest quake since 2000
Japan	3/11/2011	9.0	strongest quake ever in Japan
Japan	9/1/1923	8.0	most damaging quake ever in Japan
San Francisco, CA	4/18/1906	7.8	most famous US earthquake
China	7/27/1976	7.5	deadliest quake since 1900
Italy	12/28/1908	7.5	strongest quake measured in Europe

1900	1910	1920	1930	1940	1950	1960	1970	1980	1990	2000	2010	2020

Under the Sea

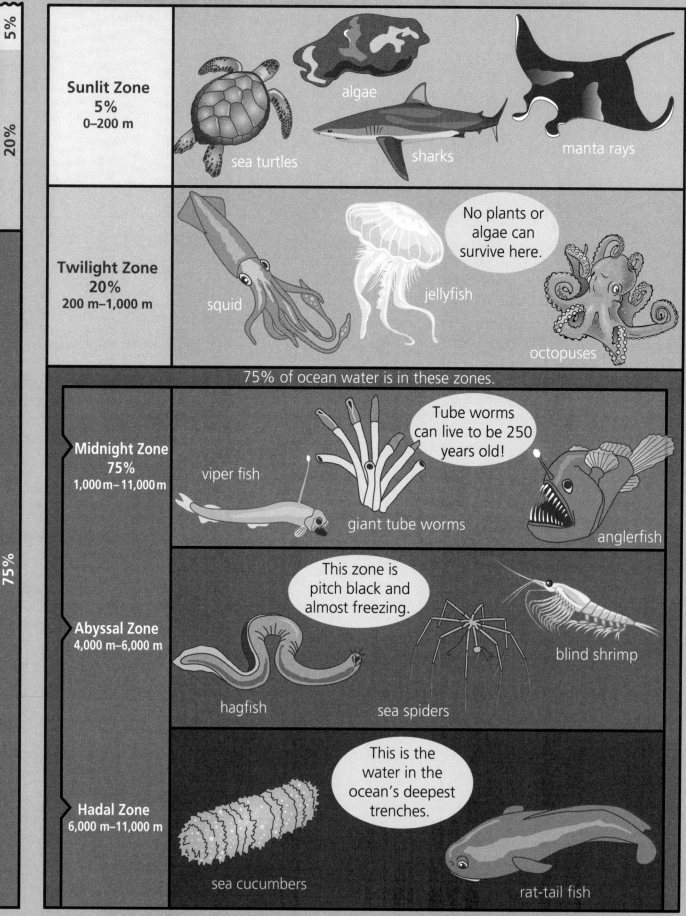

Sunlit Zone
5%
0–200 m

algae

sea turtles

sharks

manta rays

Twilight Zone
20%
200 m–1,000 m

squid

jellyfish

No plants or algae can survive here.

octopuses

75% of ocean water is in these zones.

Midnight Zone
75%
1,000 m–11,000 m

viper fish

Tube worms can live to be 250 years old!

giant tube worms

anglerfish

Abyssal Zone
4,000 m–6,000 m

This zone is pitch black and almost freezing.

hagfish

sea spiders

blind shrimp

Hadal Zone
6,000 m–11,000 m

This is the water in the ocean's deepest trenches.

sea cucumbers

rat-tail fish

5%

20%

75%

Piece It Together

Cut out each animal and glue or tape it to the diagram of sea zones on page 159. Be sure to place each creature in its correct zone underneath the ocean's surface.

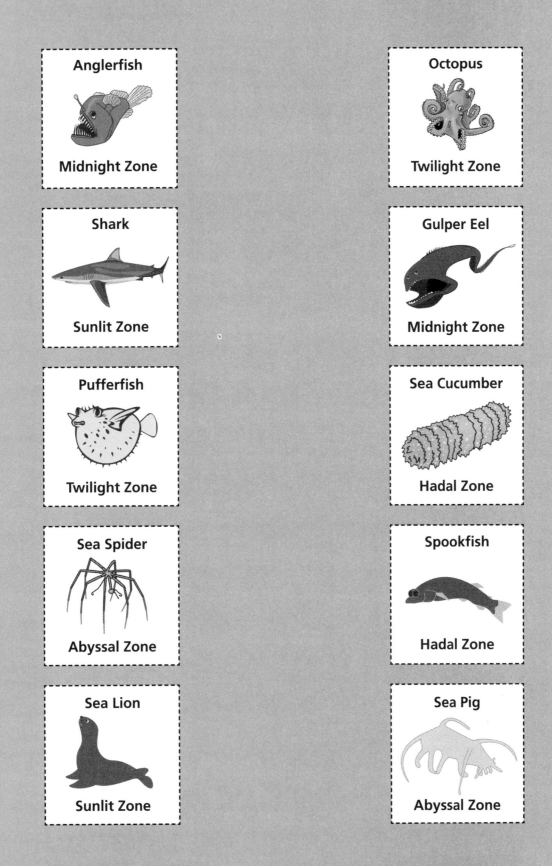

Anglerfish — Midnight Zone

Octopus — Twilight Zone

Shark — Sunlit Zone

Gulper Eel — Midnight Zone

Pufferfish — Twilight Zone

Sea Cucumber — Hadal Zone

Sea Spider — Abyssal Zone

Spookfish — Hadal Zone

Sea Lion — Sunlit Zone

Sea Pig — Abyssal Zone

Ocean Life

Sunlit Zone 0–200 m	
Twilight Zone 200 m–1,000 m	
Midnight Zone 1,000 m–11,000 m	
Abyssal Zone 4,000 m– 6,000 m	
Hadal Zone 6,000 m–11,000 m	

Talking Trash

About 12% is burned in incinerators.

In some places, garbage is used to make electricity. The trash is burned and the heat is used to turn water into steam. The steam pressure is used to power a generator that makes electricity. This is similar to the way coal is burned to make electricity.

33% gets recycled.

Trash is sorted into categories at a recycling center. Paper, plastics, bottles, and cans are sent to different places where they are broken down and turned into new materials.

55% ends up in landfills.

A landfill is not just a big hole in the ground where trash is dumped. Landfills are carefully planned so that garbage will not pollute the surrounding land or any underground sources of water.

How Long Will It Last?

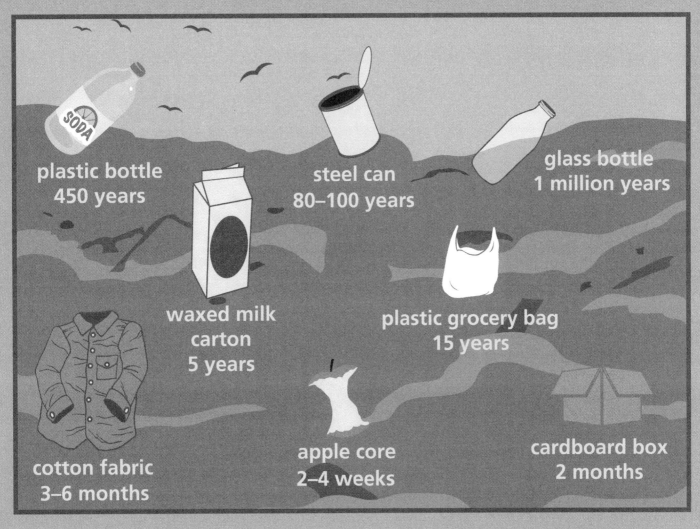

plastic bottle
450 years

steel can
80–100 years

glass bottle
1 million years

waxed milk
carton
5 years

plastic grocery bag
15 years

cotton fabric
3–6 months

apple core
2–4 weeks

cardboard box
2 months

Ways to Make Less Garbage

 Buy less (especially electronics).

 Buy things used instead of new whenever you can.

 Only take bags at a store if you need them.

 Reuse things whenever possible.

 Don't buy products that have lots of packaging.

 Sell or give away things you no longer need instead of throwing them away.

 Put your name on a "no junk mail" list to stop companies from sending you unwanted mail.

 Use rechargeable batteries.

 Whenever you can, buy bulk items at the grocery store.

 Bring your own bags to the store.

Think and Solve

Study the infographic. Answer the questions.

1. Where does most trash end up?

_____

2. True or false? A glass bottle you throw away today will still be around 100,000 years from now.

_____

3. Why is some trash burned in incinerators?

_____

4. Which of the following will last the longest in a landfill?

    A. apple core

    B. plastic bottle

    C. steel can

    D. plastic grocery bag

5. Why must landfills be planned carefully?

_____

6. What percentage of garbage is not recycled?

_____

7. Review the list of ways to create less garbage. Which do you think is the easiest to do? Which is the hardest? Explain your answers.

_____

_____

_____

Make a Pie Chart
Review the infographic. Color and label the pie chart below to show the percentage of trash that gets sent to each place: landfills, incinerators, and recycling centers.

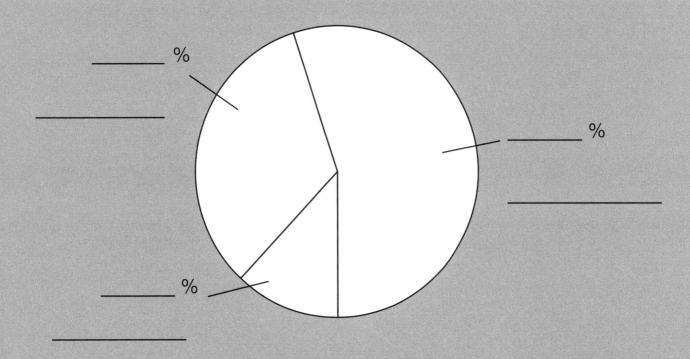

_____ %

_____

_____ %

_____

_____ %

_____

Log It
Use the log below to keep track of how much you recycle for a week. Each time you recycle one of the items shown in the first column, make a tally mark in the second column. Challenge yourself. How many marks can you make in each row during the week?

Recycled Item	Number of Items Recycled
Aluminum Can	
Steel/Tin Can	
Glass Bottle or Jar	
Plastic Bottle	
Other Plastic Container	
Cardboard or Paper Box	
Magazine/Newspaper	
Other Paper	

Ring of Fire

The Ring of Fire is made up of more than 450 volcanoes
that form a ring around the Pacific Ocean.

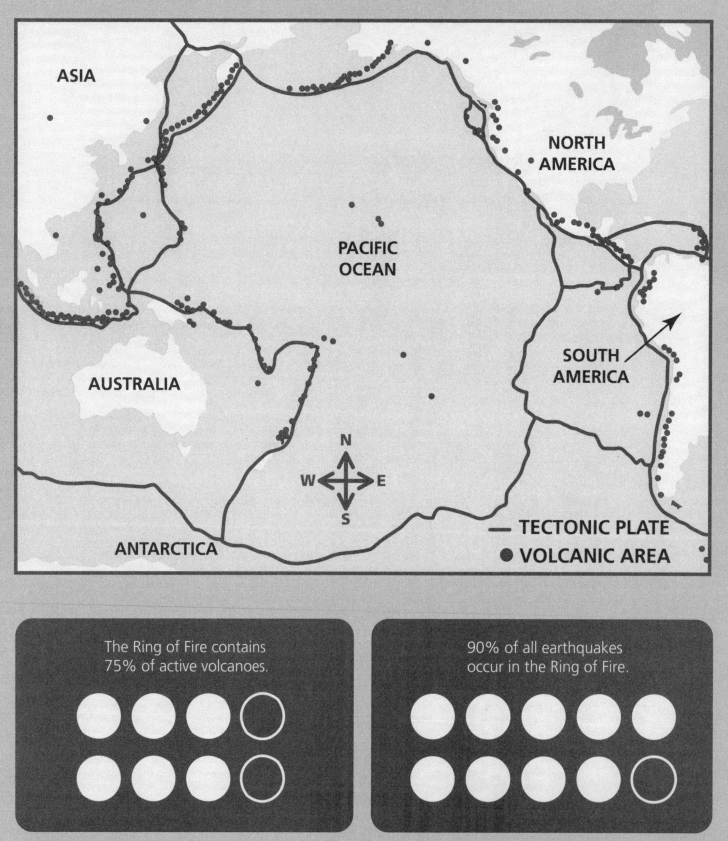

The Ring of Fire contains
75% of active volcanoes.

90% of all earthquakes
occur in the Ring of Fire.

Volcanic Eruptions That Made History

 1 **Mt. Tambora, Indonesia** (1815) This eruption made such a huge cloud of ash that there was no summer in 1816 in North America and Europe.

2 **Krakatoa, Indonesia** (1883) This explosion was more powerful than any nuclear bomb that has ever exploded.

3 **Grímsvötn, Iceland** This volcano is buried under a glacier. When it erupts, it lifts the glacier! The last eruption was in 2011.

4 **Mt. Saint Helens, Washington** (1980) This was the deadliest eruption ever in the US. Ash spewed out at nearly the speed of sound!

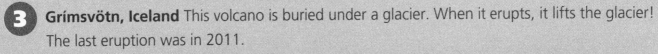

TECTONIC PLATES are part of Earth's crust. They are always shifting and moving. Sometimes, they collide or scrape against one another. The movement of these plates is the cause of earthquakes and volcanic activity in the Ring of Fire.

Think and Solve

Study the infographic. Answer the questions.

1. Name three continents with volcanoes that are part of the Ring of Fire.

_____   _____   _____

2. Why was there no summer in North America and Europe in 1816?

_____

3. On the map, Australia is _____ of North America.

   A. north and east

   B. south and west

   C. west and north

   D. east and south

4. In addition to volcanoes, what other natural event occurs along the Ring of Fire?

_____

5. True or false? Tectonic plates are fixed in place and do not move at all.

_____

6. True or false? Not all of Earth's volcanoes and earthquakes take place in the Ring of Fire.

_____

7. Which volcanic eruption was more powerful

   than any nuclear bomb that has ever exploded?

   A. Mt. Tambora, Indonesia

   B. Mt. Saint Helens, Washington

   C. Grímsvötn, Iceland

   D. Krakatoa, Indonesia

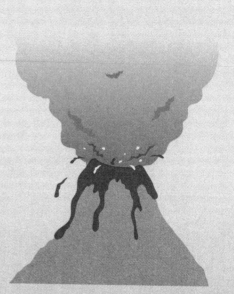

Piece It Together

Cut out the labels below. Glue or tape them to page 169 to label the parts of a volcano. The clues below will help you.

- Volcanic ash is made of rocks, minerals, and tiny bits of volcanic glass.
- *Lava* and *magma* are names for the molten hot liquid rock found in volcanoes.
- When the liquid is underground, it is called *magma*. When it flows above Earth's surface, it is called *lava*.
- A crater is the round opening at the top of a volcano.
- A vent is an opening where material flows during an eruption. Volcanoes may have more than one vent.
- A volcanic cone is a pile of lava, dust, ash, and rock that forms near a vent.

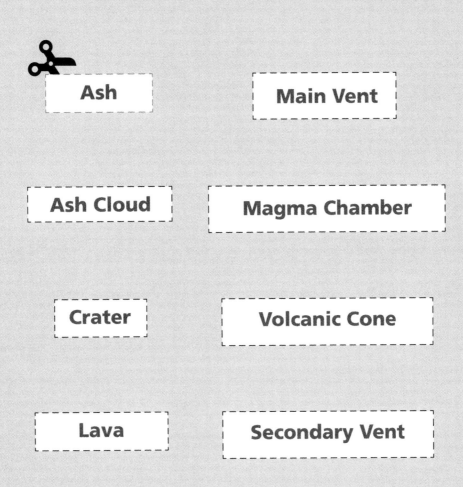

Ash	Main Vent
Ash Cloud	Magma Chamber
Crater	Volcanic Cone
Lava	Secondary Vent

A Volcano

Symbols of the United States of America

The Statue of Liberty

The statue is 305 feet tall, including the pedestal.

The Statue of Liberty was a gift to the United States from France in 1886. The statue's formal name is *Liberty Enlightening the World*.

July 4, 1776, is inscribed, or written, on the tablet she holds in her left hand.

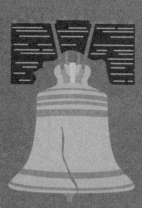

Liberty Bell

The Liberty Bell rang on July 8, 1776, to celebrate the first time the *Declaration of Independence* was read to the public.

The Liberty Bell first cracked when it was tested soon after being made in 1752. It was repaired, but it cracked again in 1835. That was the last time the Liberty Bell rang.

US Flag

One of the first US flags had 13 stars in a circle to stand for the first 13 states. As new states became part of the US, the number of stars had to be changed. There have been more than 20 versions of the flag throughout US history.

The flag can be different sizes, but the length is always 1.9 times--or almost twice--as long as it is wide.

13 STRIPES stand for the original 13 states.

50 STARS stand for the 50 states.

Great Seal of the United States

THE OLIVE BRANCH WITH 13 LEAVES stands for the power to make peace.

THE 13 ARROWS stand for the power to make war.

THE BALD EAGLE was chosen in 1782 as the symbol for the United States because of its stength, beauty, and long life.

The Star-Spangled Banner

"The Star-Spangled Banner" was a poem written by Francis Scott Key in 1814. He wrote the poem while watching ships being attacked during the War of 1812. The poem was later set to music. In 1931, it became the official anthem, or song, of the United States.

Uncle Sam

Uncle Sam is a symbol of the US government. He is often used in political cartoons. During World Wars I and II, the image of Uncle Sam was used on posters to encourage people to join the army.

Think and Solve
Study the infographic. Answer the questions.

1. There have been more than _____ different versions of the US flag.

2. Why is the number 13 important as a symbol for the United States?

_____

3. If a US flag is 12 inches wide, about how long will it be?

_____

4. What do the olive branches on the Great Seal symbolize?

   A. America's farmers

   B. the power to make peace

   C. the power to make war

   D. America's growth as a nation

5. Francis Scott Key wrote "The Star-Spangled Banner" during _____.

   A. the Revolutionary War

   B. the War of 1812

   C. the Civil War

   D. the Spanish-American War

6. True or false? Uncle Sam was one of Benjamin Franklin's nicknames.

_____

7. What is the Statue of Liberty's formal name?

_____

The Star Spangled Banner

Words: Francis Scott Key   Music: John Stafford Smith

Oh- - say! can you see, by the dawn's ear- ly

Research and Report

American coins and bills contain symbols of the United States. Some of the symbols are shown in the infographic. Others are not. Gather five different coins and bills and look for symbols on them. In the chart below, list each coin or bill and describe at least two symbols you find on it.

Coin or Bill	Symbol 1	Symbol 2

Draw and Write

Think about what is most important to you about living in the United States. What animal, object, shape, or color could you use to tell others about your ideas? In the space below, design your own symbol for the United States. On the lines, describe the symbol and explain what it means to you.

_____

_____

_____

_____

_____

_____

_____

_____

_____

_____

_____

_____

Unsinkable?

number of lifeboats on the *Titanic*

20
(there should have been 64)

882
length in feet of the *Titanic*

2 number of libraries and barber shops on the *Titanic*

1985
the year the wreck was discovered

175
height in feet of the *Titanic*

7½
amount in millions of dollars that it cost to build the *Titanic*

3 number of years it took to build the *Titanic*

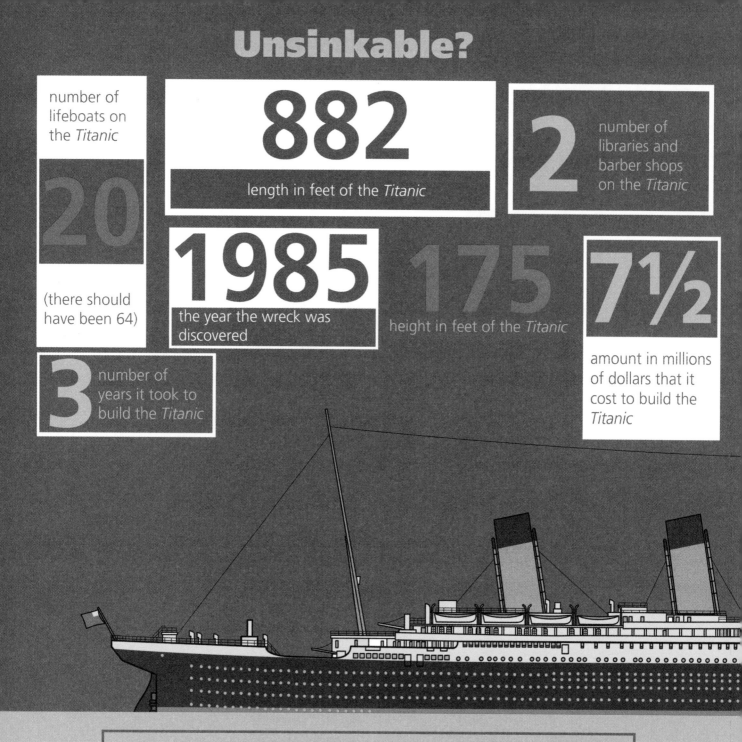

On April 10, 1912, the *Titanic* set out on its first voyage. It was traveling from England to New York City. The massive ship had been called "unsinkable." Just before midnight on April 14, the *Titanic* hit a huge iceberg. It tore a hole in the ship's hull. Less than three hours later, the *Titanic* sank. There were not enough lifeboats. About 1,500 of the passengers and crew died.

2,200
approximate number of people who set sail on the ship

14,000

gallons of drinking water used on the *Titanic* each day

100

approximate height in feet of the iceberg that sank the *Titanic*

44,000

pieces of silverware on the *Titanic*

800

tons of coal used on board each day

28

temperature of the ocean in degrees Fahrenheit the night the *Titanic* sank

15

weight in tons of each anchor on the *Titanic* (it had 2 anchors)

2½

how many miles underwater the wreck of the *Titanic* was discovered

160

number of minutes it took the *Titanic* to sink

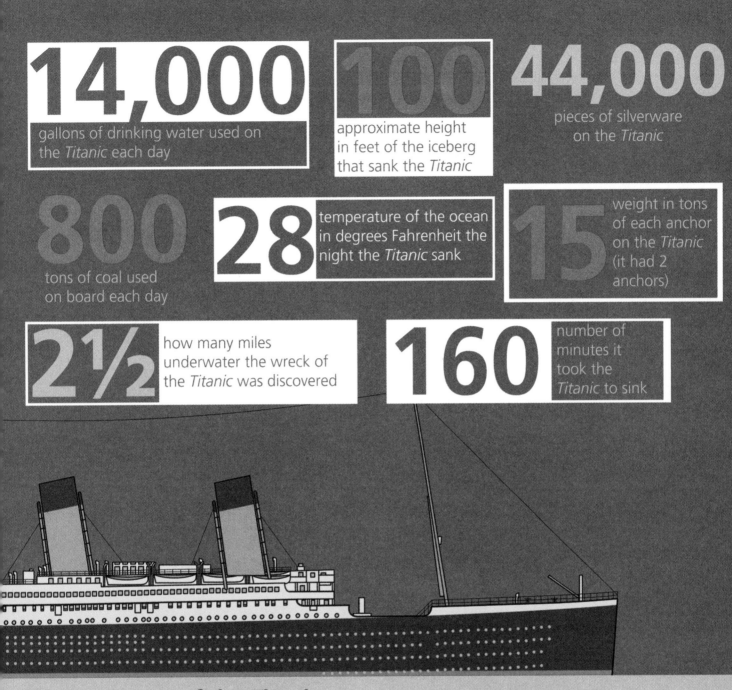

The Last Hours of the *Titanic*

April 14	11:40 P.M.	The *Titanic* strikes an iceberg.
April 14	11:50 P.M.	Water begins pouring into the *Titanic*.
April 15	12:00 A.M.	The captain gives the order to radio for help.
April 15	12:05 A.M.	The crew begins preparing the lifeboats.
April 15	12:25 A.M.	Women and children start getting into the lifeboats.
April 15	12:45 A.M.	The first lifeboat is lowered into the water.
April 15	2:05 A.M.	The last lifeboat is lowered into the water.
April 15	2:17 A.M.	The final call for help is sent over the radio.
April 15	2:20 A.M.	The *Titanic* breaks apart and sinks.
April 15	4:10 A.M.	The *Carpathia* rescues survivors from the first lifeboat.
April 15	8:50 A.M.	The *Carpathia* begins sailing to New York City with the *Titanic's* 705 survivors.

Do the Math

Solve the problems. Use the infographic to help you.

1. How much, in pounds, did each of the *Titanic*'s anchors weigh? (Hint: 1 ton = 2,000 pounds)

   A. 15,000 pounds
   B. 30,000 pounds
   C. 45,000 pounds
   D. 60,000 pounds

2. After the captain radioed for help, about how long did it take for a ship to arrive and begin rescuing passengers?

   _____

3. Write an equation that shows how to find how many years it took for the wreck of the *Titanic* to be discovered.

   _____

4. The wreck of the *Titanic* is _____ feet below the ocean's surface. (Hint: 1 mile = 5,280 feet)

   A. 1,320
   B. 10,560
   C. 13,200
   D. 250

5. Today, it would cost about 23 times as much to build the *Titanic*. Which equation could you use to find the cost of building the *Titanic* today?

   A. $7\frac{1}{2} + 23$
   B. $7\frac{1}{2} - 23$
   C. $7\frac{1}{2} \div 23$
   D. $7\frac{1}{2} \times 23$

6. True or false? The *Titanic* was supposed to have about three times more lifeboats than it did.

   _____

7. How much longer was the *Titanic* than it was tall?

   _____

Write About It

It is 1912, and the *Carpathia* is arriving in New York City with survivors from the *Titanic*. Imagine you are a reporter for the *New York News* newspaper. You have been assigned to write an article about what has happened. Use information from the infographic to write your news report on the lines below. Remember to answer the questions *Who?*, *What?*, *When?*, *Where?*, *Why?*, and *How?*

New York News

The Unsinkable Ship Has Sunk!

Titanic

...On Earth

Highest Point
Mount Everest is 8,848 m above sea level.

Lowest Point
The Mariana Trench is 10,809 m below sea level.

Hottest Place
In 1913, Death Valley reached a world-record high of 57°C (134.6°F).

Coldest Place
In part of Antarctica, the temperatures can drop to -92°C (-133.6°F).

Highest Waterfall
Angel Falls is 985 m high.

Deepest Lake
Lake Baikal is 1,637 m deep.

Largest Warm Desert
The Sahara Desert covers an area of about 9 million square km.

Largest Cold Desert
The Antarctic Polar Desert covers an area of about 14 million square km.

Largest Saltwater Lake
The Caspian Sea covers an area of 371,000 square km.

Largest Freshwater Lake
Lake Superior covers an area of 82,100 square km.

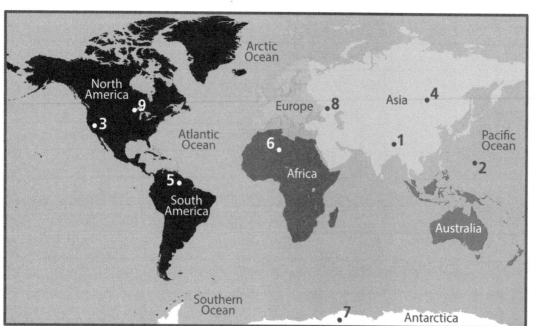

1. Mount Everest

2. Mariana Trench

3. Death Valley

4. Lake Baikal

5. Angel Falls

6. Sahara Desert

7. Antarctica

8. Caspian Sea

9. Lake Superior

Think and Solve

Study the infographic. Answer the questions.

1. If you started at the bottom of Lake Baikal and traveled up above the water to the same height as Angel Falls, how far would you go?

_____meters

2. Which place mentioned in the infographic is located in Africa?

_____

3. Rounded to the nearest thousand, Lake Superior covers an area of _____ square kilometers.

A. 80,000

B. 82,000

C. 85,000

D. 100,000

4. True or false? The hottest place on Earth is the Sahara Desert.

_____

5. The Antarctic Polar Desert is_____square kilometers bigger than the Sahara.

6. Look at the words in the infographic that have the ending -*est*. In your own words, tell what the ending means.

_____

_____

Explore Your World

Use the Internet or another resource to find out the following about your town or city.

The highest point: _____   How high is it? _____

The tallest building: _____   How tall is it? _____

The biggest park: _____   How big is it? _____

The biggest lake or other body of water: _____   How big is it? _____

The average temperature in July: _____

The average temperature in January: _____

Answer Key

Page 7

Think and Solve
Study the infographic. Answer the questions.

1. How many more decibels louder is an ambulance siren than a refrigerator?
   A. 140 dB
   B. 120 dB
   C. 80 dB
   D. 100 dB

2. The noise of a circular saw is 100 decibels. According to the US Occupational Safety and Health Act of 1970, what is the maximum number of hours a day you should use a circular saw?
   2 hours

3. Prolonged exposure to city traffic can cause hearing loss.
   True   False

4. Give an example of noise pollution. Explain why the noise is a kind of pollution.
   Answers will vary but should include a description of noise pollution as unwanted and/or irritating noise.

5. Where do you think the sound of a rocket launch would be placed on the graph?
   Answers will vary but may include at or above the noise of a firecracker (150 dB).

Estimate It
Go outside and listen. What do you hear? List the sounds on the lines.
Color the bar to estimate the decibels for each sound.

Information will vary.

DECIBELS   5 15 25 35 45 55 65 75 85 95 105 115 125 135 150

Page 7

Page 10

Do the Math
Study the infographic. Solve the problems.

1. How much taller would a stack of 2,000,000 dollar bills be than the Statue of Liberty?
   A. 53 feet
   B. 106 feet
   C. 252 feet
   D. 411 feet

2. About how many one-dollar bills are printed in five days?
   A. 16 million
   B. 48 million
   C. 64 million
   D. 80 million

3. What percentage of bills printed in the US are five- and ten-dollar bills?
   17%

4. How much less does one million dollars weigh in ten-dollar bills than in one-dollar bills?
   1,836 pounds

5. Is the average dollar bill in circulation for more or less than two years?
   less

Make a Chart
Gather five different coins and bills. Look at the money carefully, noticing details. Then, use the chart below to record information about each coin or bill. Write its value, the date that appears on it, the name of the person whose portrait appears on it, and one more detail.

Money Type	Value	Date	Portrait	Another Detail
Information will vary.				

Page 10

Page 14

Think and Solve
Study the infographic. Answer the questions.

1. What does the dog sled command easy mean?
   A. turn right
   B. turn left
   C. slow down
   D. stop

2. If a race team is racing on the southern route, where is the halfway checkpoint?
   Eagle Island

3. What happened during the Great Race of Mercy?
   A. A team of mushers delivered medicine to Nome, Alaska, in rough winter weather.
   B. A team of mushers had to deliver mail to Willow, Alaska, in icy conditions.
   C. A team of mushers raced each other to win money for a charity.
   D. none of the above

4. Diphtheria is a type of   illness

5. Would you like to be on a race team in the Iditarod? Why or why not?
   Answers will vary.

Write About It
Imagine that you are a contestant in the Iditarod. Write a journal entry about your experience on one day of the race.
Journal entries will vary.

Page 14

Page 17

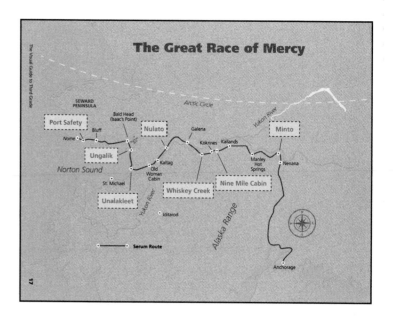

Page 17

Page 21

Study the infographic and read the passage on page 20. Answer the questions.

1. Who designed the Niagara Falls Power Plant?
Nikola Tesla

2. Goat Island is located between ___Bridal Veil Falls___ and ___Horseshoe Falls___.

3. Where does the water come from that feeds Niagara Falls?
A. from the Atlantic Ocean
B. from Hudson Bay
(C. from the Great Lakes)
D. from the Pacific Ocean

4. During peak flow, about how much water pours over the falls in one minute?
A. 420,000 gallons
B. 700,000 gallons
(C. 42,000,000 gallons)
D. 700,000,000 gallons

5. About how many people visit Niagara Falls each year?
thirty million people

6. Number the steps 1–5 to show the order used to create hydroelectric power.
___3___ The turbine spins an electric generator.
___1___ Swiftly moving water flows into a tunnel.
___5___ Electricity flows through wires to power buildings and machines.
___2___ The force of the water turns a turbine.
___4___ The generator uses wires and magnets to create electricity.

7. Use what you know about hydroelectricity to describe how a windmill is used to create electricity.
Answers will vary but should describe how the wind spins the blades, which are connected to an electrical generator.

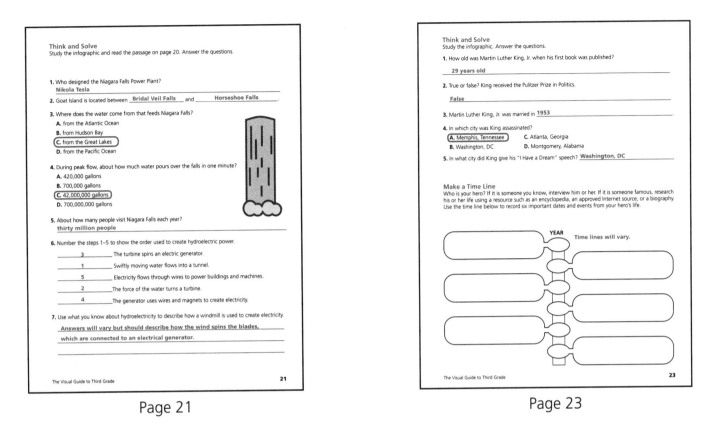

Page 21

Page 23

Study the infographic. Answer the questions.

1. How old was Martin Luther King, Jr. when his first book was published?
29 years old

2. True or false? King received the Pulitzer Prize in Politics.
False

3. Martin Luther King, Jr. was married in ___1953___.

4. In which city was King assassinated?
(A. Memphis, Tennessee)   C. Atlanta, Georgia
B. Washington, DC   D. Montgomery, Alabama

5. In what city did King give his "I Have a Dream" speech? Washington, DC

Make a Time Line
Who is your hero? If it is someone you know, interview him or her. If it is someone famous, research his or her life using a resource such as an encyclopedia, an approved Internet source, or a biography. Use the time line below to record six important dates and events from your hero's life.

YEAR   Time lines will vary.

Page 23

Page 26

Study the infographic. Answer the questions.

1. Where is the Graveyard of the Atlantic?
A. off the coast of South Carolina
(B. off the coast of North Carolina)
C. off the coast of Virginia
D. all of the above

2. Diamond Shoals is a _____.
A. coral reef
B. famous shipwreck
(C. sandbar)
D. city

3. How many feet longer was the *Proteus* than the USS *Atlanta*?
186 feet

4. Which boat sank in 1862?
USS Monitor

5. Blackbeard, Black Bart, and Calico Jack were all part of the same crew.
True (False)

6. What shipwreck occurred in 1718?
Blackbeard's ship Queen Anne's Revenge

7. During which war did German U-boats sink 60 ships?
World War I

8. Nags Head is north of Corolla.
True (False)

9. Why does the time line go back only as far as the year 1500?
Ships did not commonly sail in the area earlier than 1500.

10. Why is the area near the coast nicknamed "The Graveyard of the Atlantic"?
because it is a dangerous area in the ocean where thousands of shipwrecks have happened

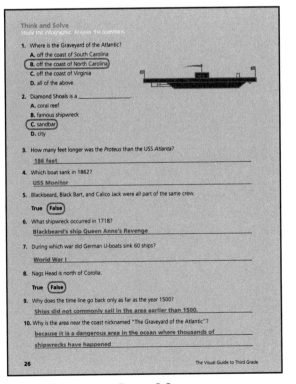

Page 26

Page 29

A Pirate Ship

Main Mast
Foremast
Mizzenmast
Quarterdeck
Bowsprit
Rudder
Figurehead
Gun Port
Hull
Keel

Page 29

Page 34

Read About It:
STATE STORIES

HOW DID STATES GET THEIR NICKNAMES? Some are obvious. Delaware is called "The First State" because it was the first state to sign the US Constitution. Rhode Island's nickname, "The Ocean State," makes sense because Rhode Island is right beside the Atlantic Ocean. Other state nicknames have a story behind them. Alaska has several nicknames. One is "Land of the Midnight Sun." Because Alaska is located so far north, for part of the year, the sun never sets completely. It is light 24 hours a day, even at midnight! Alaska is also known as "Seward's Folly." Secretary of State William Seward made the deal to purchase Alaska from Russia in 1867. It was so cold, wild, and isolated that many people thought the purchase was a *folly*, or foolish idea.

Categorize It
Write state nicknames for each category.

1. Write three state nicknames that include animals.

   Answers will vary but may include: Beaver State, Badger State, Pelican State

2. Write two state nicknames that include the word *sun*.

   Sunshine State   **Sunflower State**

3. Write three state nicknames that include bodies of water.

   Bay State   **Ocean State**   **Great Lakes State**

4. Which state is nicknamed after a fruit?

   Georgia

5. Write two state nicknames that include metals.

   Golden State

   Silver State

Alaska
The Last Frontier or Land of the Midnight Sun

Page 35

Label It
Spend a few minutes studying the map on pages 32–33.
Then, see how many state names you can fill in on the map below. Answer the questions.

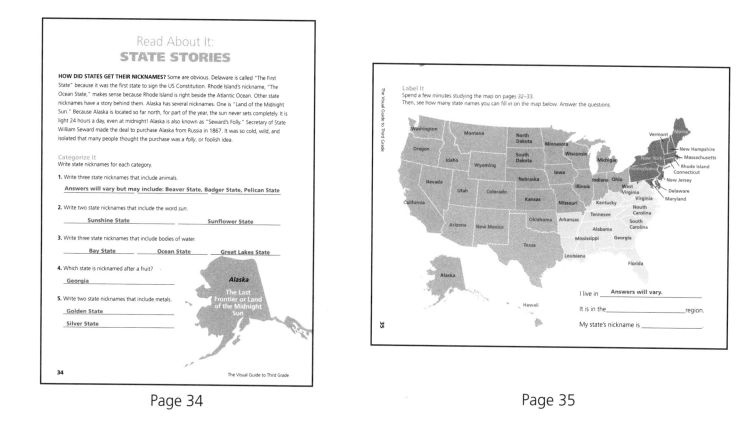

I live in _____**Answers will vary.**_____

It is in the _____ region.

My state's nickname is _____.

Page 38

Think and Solve
Study the infographic. Answer the questions.

1. There are more than 30 million plant specimens at the Museum of Natural History.

   True   (**False**)

2. Which direction would you walk to go from the National Gallery of Art to the Smithsonian Air and Space Museum?

   A. north and west
   B. east and south
   (**C.** south and west)
   D. west and north

3. Which museum would you visit if you wanted to learn more about astronauts?

   Smithsonian Air and Space Museum

4. The National Gallery Sculpture Garden is inside the National Gallery of Art.

   True   (**False**)

5. In what year did construction begin on the Washington Monument?

   1848

Schedule It
Plan a day of sightseeing along the National Mall. Keep in mind that each museum has many things to look at. You will not be able to see everything in one day! Choose which places you most want to visit and how long you will spend at each one. Don't forget to include time for lunch! Write your plan on the schedule below.

	Schedules will vary.		
8:00 A.M.		2:00 P.M.	
9:00 A.M.		3:00 P.M.	
10:00 A.M.		4:00 P.M.	
11:00 A.M.		5:00 P.M.	
12:00 P.M.		6:00 P.M.	
1:00 P.M.		7:00 P.M.	

Page 46

Do the Math
Study the infographic. Solve the problems.

1. The Amazon River and the Paraná River are in South America. How many combined miles of the longest rivers run through South America?

   7,032 miles

2. How much longer is the Nile than the Mekong River?

   1,555 miles

3. True or false? The Nile is more than twice as long as the Mississippi River.

   False

4. How far is it from the source of the Niger River to the mouth of the Niger River?

   2,597 miles

5. True or false? The infographic shows the lengths of 10 rivers.

   False

Explore Your World
Ask an adult to take you to a river near your home. Sit quietly and observe the area for several minutes. Draw the river in the box below. Then, use the lines to record your observations.

Observations will vary.

What I Saw: _____

What I Heard: _____

What I Smelled: _____

What I Felt: _____

Drawings will vary.

Page 34   Page 35

Page 38   Page 46

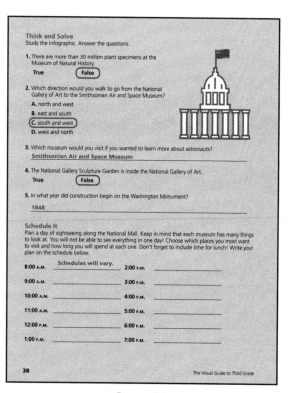

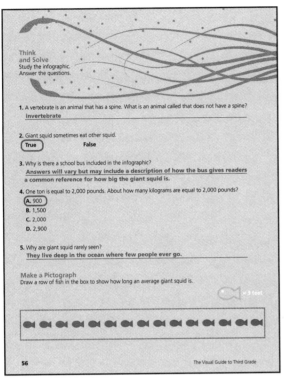

Page 56

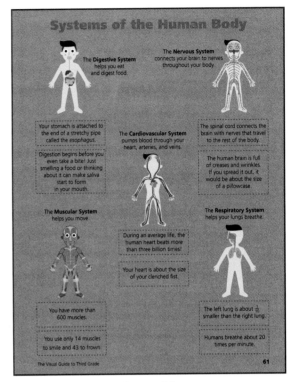

Page 61

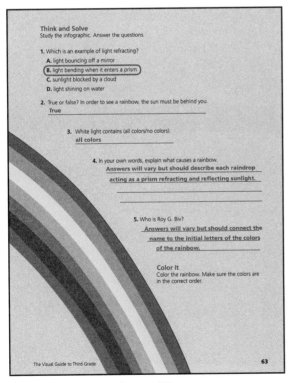

Page 63

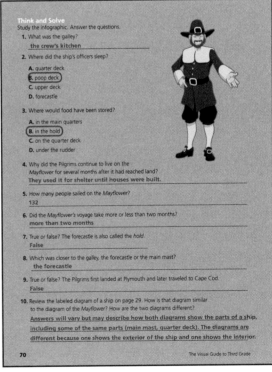

Page 70

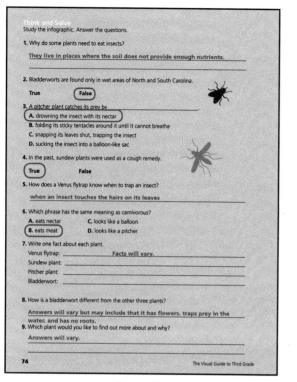

Page 74

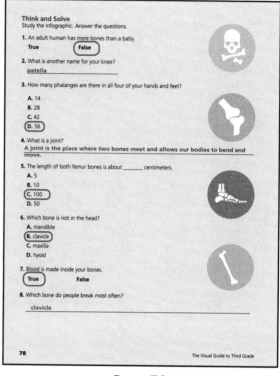

Page 78

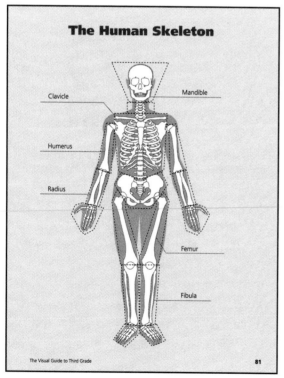

Page 81

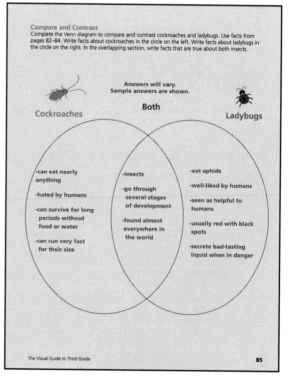

Page 85

Page 88

Think and Solve
Study the infographic. Answer the questions.

1. True or false? The first color TV was shown at the 1939 World's Fair.
   False

2. Why was cable TV invented?
   A. to make the pictures look better
   B. to add sound to the pictures shown on TV
   C. to bring TV to people who could not get a signal
   D. to send pictures more quickly

3. The first satellite images were broadcast _____14_____ years after cable TV was invented.

4. At least _____ American homes had a TV in 1950.
   A. five million   C. fifty million
   B. three and a half million   D. four and a half million

Log It   Logs will vary.
How much TV do you watch in one week? Use the chart below to keep track of the time you spend watching TV each day for a week. Round the amount of time to the nearest $\frac{1}{2}$ hour.

Day	Hours of TV Watching
Sunday	
Monday	
Tuesday	
Wednesday	
Thursday	
Friday	
Saturday	
Total for the Week:	

Do you think you spend too much time watching TV? Why or why not?
Answers will vary.

List activities you might choose to do instead of watching TV.

Page 88

Page 89

Read About It:
How We Watch

TODAY, THERE ARE MANY CHOICES OF HOW TO WATCH TV. You might watch your favorite show on a computer, on a tablet, or on a 3-D television screen. But just 25 years ago, the choices were much more limited. Then, most families could watch only what was showing on a broadcast channel or cable channel. By the year 2000, nearly every home in the US had a VCR, or videocassette recorder and player. These devices allowed people to purchase or record shows and movies and choose when to watch them. DVDs and Blu-ray discs continued this trend. In 2002, more DVD players were sold than VCRs. By 2004, people had more choices than ever—there were more than 300 cable TV channels to choose from! Internet streaming services such as Netflix began in 2008, bringing even more TV-watching choices.

The devices we call TVs have also gone through many changes over time. In 1990, TVs were shaped like big, square boxes. The first widescreen, or rectangular, TVs went on sale in 1993. Two years later, the first flat-screen TVs became available. Today, most TV is shown in HDTV, or high-definition television. The picture is very clear and bright. The first show broadcast in HDTV was in 1998.

Make a Time Line
On the time line, write events described in the passage above. Draw a line from each event to the place on the time line that shows the year it happened.

	1990	
TVs are big square boxes		Widescreen TVs
	1995	
HDTV		Flat-screen TVs
	2000	
Almost all homes have a VCR		DVD outsells VCR
	2005	
More than 300 cable channels	2010	Streaming begins

Page 89

Page 93

Make Idea Webs
Read the adjective in the center of each web. On the lines, write facts and examples from Ben Franklin's life that show how the adjective describes him.

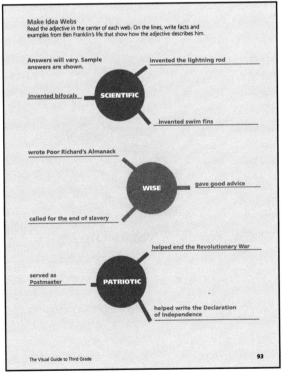

Answers will vary. Sample answers are shown.

invented the lightning rod
invented bifocals
SCIENTIFIC
invented swim fins

wrote Poor Richard's Almanack
WISE
gave good advice
called for the end of slavery

helped end the Revolutionary War
served as Postmaster
PATRIOTIC
helped write the Declaration of Independence

Page 93

Page 96

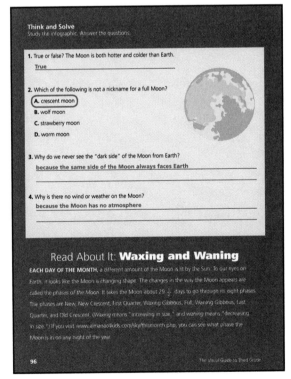

Think and Solve
Study the infographic. Answer the questions.

1. True or false? The Moon is both hotter and colder than Earth.
   True

2. Which of the following is not a nickname for a full Moon?
   A. crescent moon
   B. wolf moon
   C. strawberry moon
   D. worm moon

3. Why do we never see the "dark side" of the Moon from Earth?
   because the same side of the Moon always faces Earth

4. Why is there no wind or weather on the Moon?
   because the Moon has no atmosphere

Read About It: Waxing and Waning

EACH DAY OF THE MONTH, a different amount of the Moon is lit by the Sun. To our eyes on Earth, it looks like the Moon is changing shape. The changes in the way the Moon appears are called the *phases of the Moon*. It takes the Moon about 29 $\frac{1}{2}$ days to go through its eight phases. The phases are New, New Crescent, First Quarter, Waxing Gibbous, Full, Waning Gibbous, Last Quarter, and Old Crescent. (*Waxing* means "increasing in size," and *waning* means "decreasing in size.") If you visit www.almanac4kids.com/sky/thismonth.php, you can see what phase the Moon is in on any night of the year.

Page 96

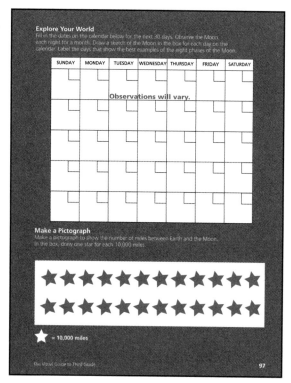

Page 97

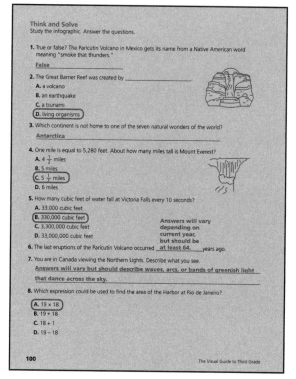

Page 100

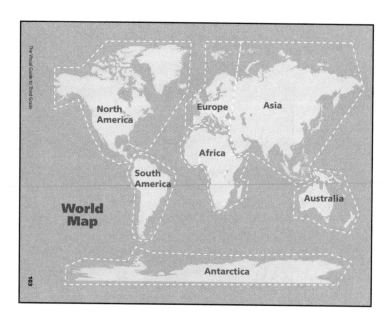

Page 103

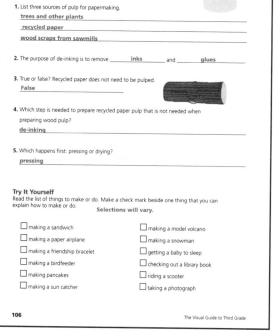

Page 106

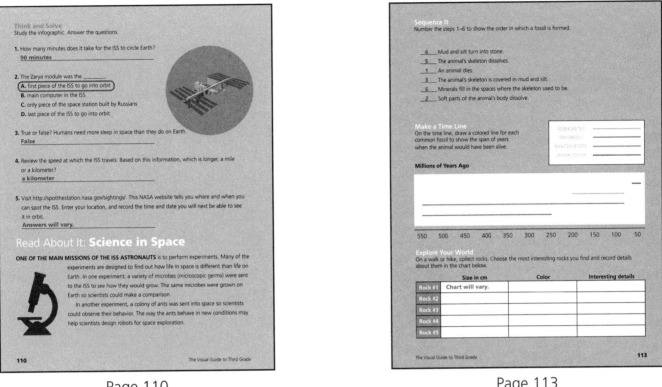

Page 110

Page 113

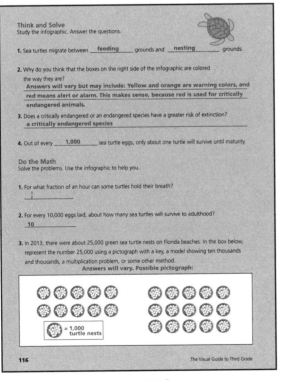

Page 116

Page 117

Page 124

Think and Solve
Study the infographic. Answer the questions.

1. The first summer Olympics were held in Greece in the year 1896

2. How are the flags of Sweden and Finland similar and different?
They both have the same cross-like design. Sweden is blue with a yellow
cross, and Finland's is white with a blue cross.

3. Why were the Olympics canceled in 1916, 1940, and 1944?
because of wars

4. True or false? France and Germany have each hosted the Olympics two times.
False

Categorize It
Read the list of Olympic events. Write each event under the correct category.

tennis	fencing	sailing	biathlon
diving	golf	alpine skiing	volleyball
snowboarding	figure skating	ice hockey	rowing
football	judo	triathlon	taekwondo
swimming	pentathlon	basketball	

Events That Use a Ball

tennis   football
basketball   volleyball
golf

Martial Arts

fencing   judo
taekwondo

Events That Take Place in the Water

swimming   rowing
diving   sailing

Events That Take Place on Ice or Snow

figure skating   snowboarding
alpine skiing   ice hockey

Events That Involve More Than One Sport

biathlon   triathlon   pentathlon

Page 125

Map It
This map shows the continents of the world. Use the infographic to make a tally mark on a continent each time a country on that continent has hosted the Olympics. If you are not sure on what continent a country is found, use a globe, an atlas, or an online map to look it up. (Note: The country of Russia was once known as the USSR. It spans two continents. Count it in both.)

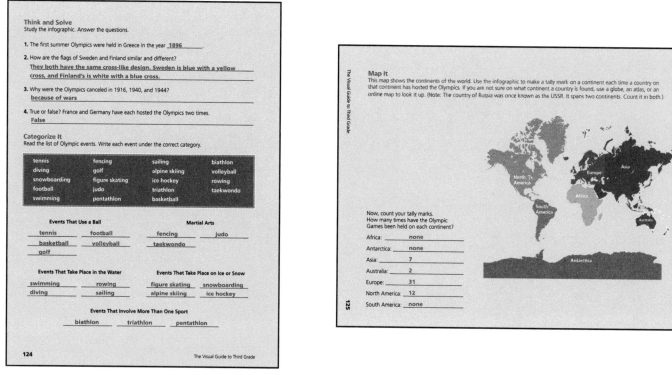

Now, count your tally marks.
How many times have the Olympic
Games been held on each continent?

Africa: none
Antarctica: none
Asia: 7
Australia: 2
Europe: 31
North America: 12
South America: none

Page 128

Think and Solve
Study the infographic. Answer the questions.

1. One mile is equal to 5,280 feet. Measured in miles, about how high did Amelia Earhart fly when she set her record for flying height in 1922?
A. 1 mile
B. $2\frac{1}{2}$ miles
C. 3 miles
D. $4\frac{1}{2}$ miles

2. The search for Amelia covered 250,000 square miles. Why did it cover such a large area?
because no one knew exactly where the plane went down

3. List three countries Amelia Earhart flew over during her attempt to circle the globe.
Answers will vary but may include
Thailand,   Senegal,   Venezuela

4. True or false? Amelia Earhart was the first woman to receive an international pilot's license.
False

5. How many years passed between Amelia's first flying lesson and her disappearance?
16 years

6. How many miles of Amelia's total journey were not completed? Use the pictograph below to answer. 7,000 miles

Amelia's Final Flight

= 1,000 miles completed

= 1,000 miles not completed

Page 132

Think and Solve
Study the infographic. Answer the questions.

1. What do adult honeybees eat?
A. pollen   C. nectar
B. honey   D. The infographic does not have this information.

2. True or false? Honey that was made hundreds of years ago can still be eaten.
True

3. When would a worker bee be fed royal jelly?
when the queen bee dies

4. What is a drone?
A. a worker bee   C. a young bee
B. a queen bee that has been fed royal jelly   D. a male bee

5. What are pollen pockets?
places on a worker bee's legs that are used to store pollen

Do the Math
Solve the problems. Use the infographic to help you.

1. A honeybee hovers in the air for 8 seconds. About how many times does it flap its wings?
1,600 times

2. Which expression shows how many fewer honeybee colonies there are today than in the 1940s?
A. 5,000,000 × 2   C. 5,000,000 − $\frac{1}{2}$
B. 5,000,000 ÷ 2   D. 5,000,000 + $\frac{1}{2}$

3. A queen bee lays around 1,500 eggs per day. How many eggs does she lay in a week?
10,500 eggs

4. A hive produces 30 pounds of honey. The beekeeper takes 25 pounds of honey to sell. Which fraction shows how much of the total honey is taken by the beekeeper?
A. $\frac{6}{5}$ C. $\frac{2}{3}$
B. $\frac{5}{6}$ D. $\frac{30}{25}$

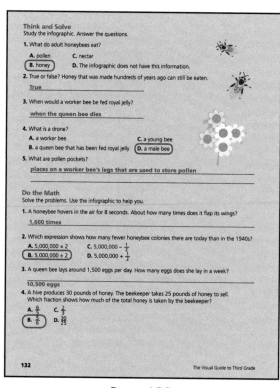

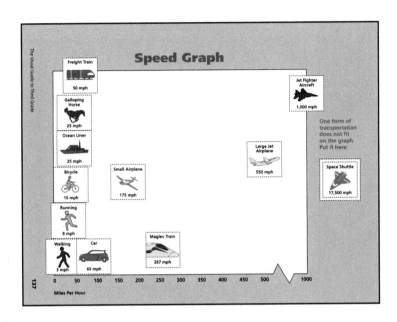

Page 137

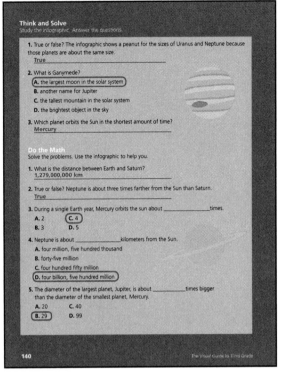

Page 140

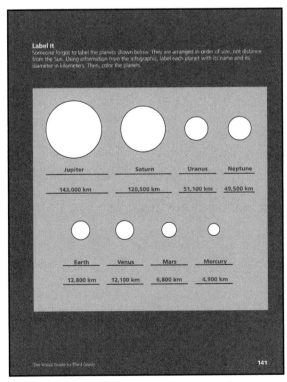

Page 141

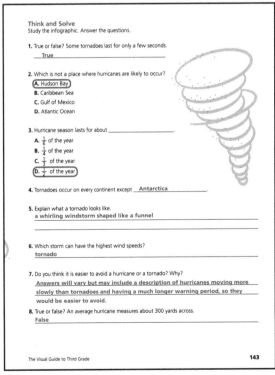

Page 143

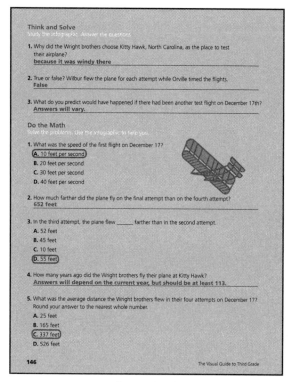

Page 146

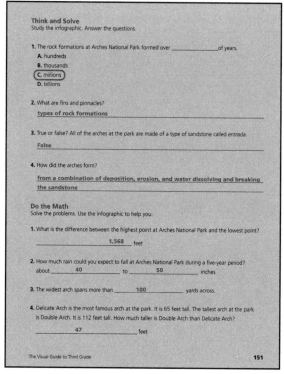

Page 151

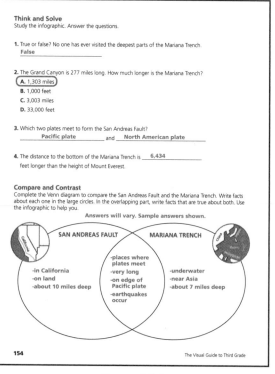

Page 154

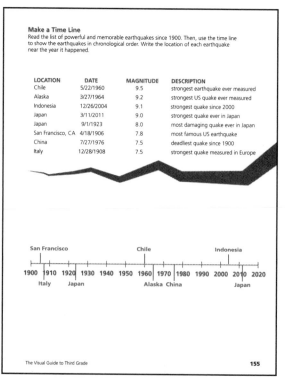

Page 155

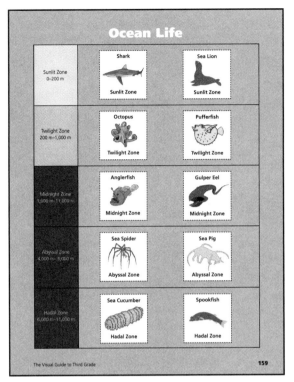

Page 159

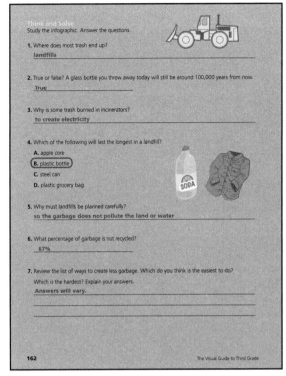

Page 162

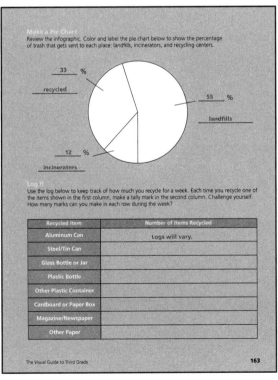

Page 163

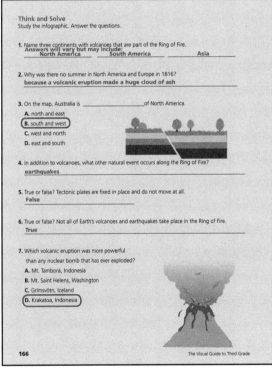

Page 166

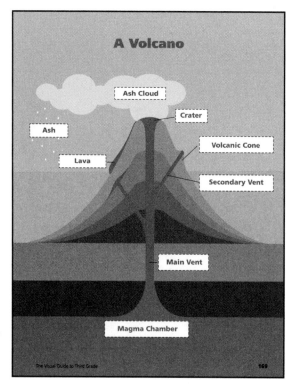

Page 169

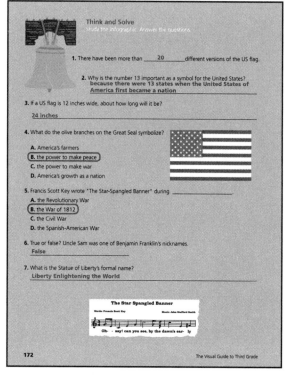

Page 172

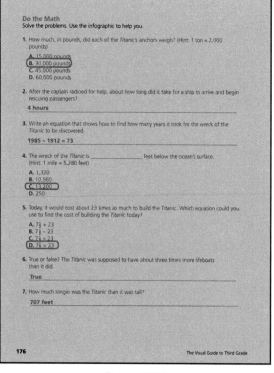

Page 176

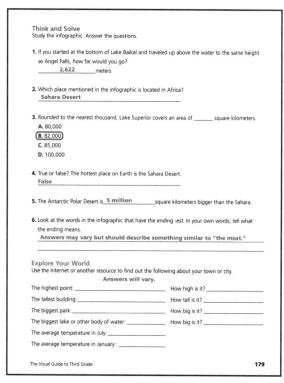

Page 179